Copyright © 2021 Tekkan
Artwork Copyright © 2021

All rights reserved.
First Printing, 2021
ISBN 978-1-7363537-4-5

To contact Tekkan please email:
buddhaboy1289@gmail.com

Table of Contents

Everyday Mind XVI . . . . Page 1

Everyday Mind XVII. . . . . Page 101

Work Shop Talk. . . . . Page 170

Everyday Mind XVIII . . . . Page 201

Dino Derby . . . . Page 222

Clouds . . . . Page 258

Tyrannosaurs in Requiem . . . . . . Page 288

Everyday Mind XIX . . . . Page 301

Everyday Mind XX . . . . Page 401

How to Read My Poems

I want to be direct in my meaning — I want people to clearly understand my meaning. My wordiness is inspired by Shakespeare, and the (aimed-for) concision is in imitation of Japanese style. Using the sonnet with the tanka, I mix the sensibility of the Occident and the Orient — which I have done by living in England, Japan, and America.

I have married the sonnet to the tanka. Often, I don't rhyme my sonnets, because I want freer expression. I tell a story in the sonnet — using three quatrains separated by line spaces, and a final couplet. The story builds to a conclusion in the couplet. The tanka is a commentary, or a counterpoint, to the sonnet — the combined poems have two endings.

Recently I have added limericks, doggerel, and rhymed sonnets into my repertoire. The limericks have a rhyme scheme but the tanka do not.

I don't punctuate much in my poetry. I want the words themselves to do the work. There is logic between words, and the forms provide structure. By not using punctuation I hope to direct readers to carefully attend to each word — to appreciate the graininess of words.

Reading my poems silently and reading them aloud may be different experiences. The way I've written, there's not always a pause intended at the end of the line.

Hint: *My poems are to be recited not as lines but as phrases, and a phrase often overflows the break at the end of a line. I pause and take a breath where it seems natural for me to pause. Another person may pause differently than I do.*

Each poem is a piece of a mosaic, and it is my hope that the collection of poems forms an accurate portrait of consciousness.

My daughter, *Jocelyn MacDonald*, is a wonderful artist. Her artwork graces this book.

I am Barry MacDonald. I received the *dharma* name *Tekkan*, which means "Iron Man," a settled practitioner of great determination.

— *Tekkan*

Everyday Mind XVI

The milder sunlight
on the verge of autumn
makes the evanescence
of the southward clouds
vivid.

I empathize with the frantic squirrel
In the necessity of the moment
In the middle of vigorous action
And suddenly seized with indecision

When seemingly it's gone too far to turn
Around and yet safety is beyond reach
As it's wavering halfway across the
Street not knowing whether to keep going

Or to go back and it must decide or
Be smooched by the tires of my car while
I understand because it happens to
Me that if I could only calm myself

Before taking action then I wouldn't
Have to rush about like an idiot.

Inattention
and
distraction
lead
to
panic.

I noticed a growth of weeds rising from
The gutters of my house and I retrieved
A ladder for an inspection and found
The wire mesh installed twelve years ago

Was useless for keeping the gutters clear
Of debris and that the gutters on two
Sides of my house were entirely clogged
While the wire mesh was resolutely

Screwed into place so I decided that
The mesh is doing me no good and I
Unscrewed it and reached under it scraping
My arms in the process of clearing the

Debris while swearing at the contractor
Who had bamboozled me twelve years ago.

After a rainstorm
I noticed debris around
the ends of the downspouts
demonstrating that
the gutters are working.

I am getting better at ascending
The arduous hill into Houlton on
My bicycle as I'm able to use
A faster gear and to sprint to the top

And whether I'm facing a headwind or
Being pushed by the wind I'm finding that
Maintaining a steady rapid cadence
Makes the distance go by quickly and these

Mild sunny afternoon rides are fodder
For a peaceful mind as there is enough
Of the sunlight — and not too much — to make
Everything golden and on the decline

Into Stillwater I am hearing a
Chorus of crickets chirping from the grass.

My
ears
and
crickets
are
inspiration.

Kitcat is a mischievous nut case
And he takes the frilly pink sponge that's called
A buf puf from the bathtub in his teeth
And he trots to my bedroom dangling

The sponge by its cord and he drops it in
Front of my door just to mess with me so
This morning I caught him dozing on the
Couch on his back in between sleeping and

Wakefulness and I took his rear paw and
Pulled and pushed it with my hand while humming
A nonsensical tune testing whether
I could keep him suspended between a

Desire for sleep and a feral urge to
Retaliate by lunging and biting.

Kitcat was a little too
drowsy to rouse himself
but he made some
lazy gestures.

I know that plastic flamingoes are not
Examples of especially fine art
And that some people disparage them by
Using the words crass or hideous in

Description of them but I believe such
Valuations are unjust and signal
The traits of superficiality
And impetuousness in the critics

As these people are only capable
Of seeing plastic objects clashing with
Their surroundings but I see delightful
Exquisite elegant magnificent

Flamingoes that are paragons of the
Creative variety of being.

Imagining the
real flamingoes
is a tasteful
exercise.

It is ninety-three million miles away
This morning and I can see it among
The maple leaves outside of my window
As a disk of blazing light and now and

Then an intervening cloud is dimming
Its brilliance and now I can only see
The maple leaves in a boisterous wind
And now I am seeing the clouds clearing

Again revealing radiance as the
Sun is ascending from the horizon
While it's astounding to remember that
Such a normal sight everyone has seen

Is really an illusion as the sun
Isn't rising but the earth is spinning.

The earth is spinning
on its axis
toward the sun at
one thousand miles per hour.

I am well aware that these sunny days
Will not last and I won't be able to
Ride my bicycle in shorts and short sleeves
For very much longer and I really

Do love these afternoons of crickets and
Wildflowers while I'm pumping my legs in
A rapid cadence doing my circuit
Over two bridges around the river

Valley again and again while there's a
Guy I'm seeing quite often walking on
The same trail bare-chested and wearing shorts
And I've passed him at least a dozen times

And every time he's staring at his phone
Oblivious to summer majesty.

Somehow he follows the trail
walking while hypnotized
by the screen of his
smartphone.

I'm seeing monarch butterflies while I
Am repeating my twenty-mile circuit
On my bicycle and I recognize
These are the super generation of

Monarchs that will migrate three thousand miles
From North America to the mountains
In central Mexico to winter in
Temperate weather among what are called

Sacred fir trees and I'm wondering how
Do they understand to make use of
Air currents and how do the different
Groups of migrants every autumn arrive

Repeatedly at the sacred mountains
When they will only make the journey once?

Will these monarchs
I am seeing today
follow currents over
the Grand Canyon and
the Colorado River?

I experience the times of the day
When my energy is diminished and
I also understand that I indulge
Currents of thought that reinforce why my

Circumstances are difficult which leads
Me to wallow in self-pity and I'm
Aware such attitudes are extremely
Unattractive to others because in

Secret most us harbor these gloomy
Sorts of ruminations and when I am
Grumpy it's hard to empathize with you
While I'm expressing quiet aggression

But I also know that the mood will pass
And I will be exuberant again.

Energy and
enthusiasm
reliably
come
together.

It is possible to take pleasure in
The phantasmagoria of the earth
Mixing DNA and protoplasm
That produces a platypus and

Maybe a scientist could offer a
Hypothesis but I am thinking that
He would discount the child like wonderment
That no matter how world-weary I am

Enchantment can be tasted everywhere
And with an impish imagination
I can drop an empty snail shell inside
A tuba a chubby high school freshman

Is sounding in a concert and picture
Curves within curves within resonation.

Do you suppose an
empty snail shell inside
a tuba a chubby boy
is blowing would
rattle?

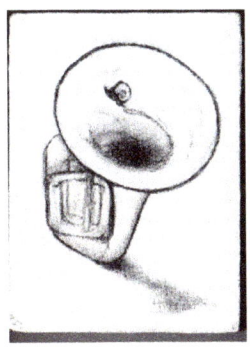

I would think a person would have to be
Crazy to stand on a mountain wearing
A wing suit facing the spectacular
Void of air and distance resolved to jump

Remembering as I do the ancient
Fable of *Icarus* who flew too close
To the sun with the sun melting his wings
Of wax and feathers causing him to fall

While obviously modern nylon is
More reliable than wax and feathers
It would take a lusting for excitement
And a courageous recklessness to leap

Slicing air within the precipices
Enraptured in the ecstasy of flight.

Most of us settle for
a window seat
on an airliner
with peanut snacks.

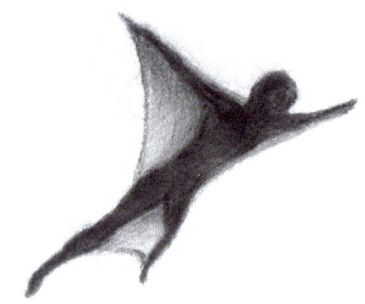

I take comfort in the contemplation
Of the way that the cosmos works in that
Gravity forms clouds of gases into
The suns and planets and that cyclical

Motion in the form of elliptical
Orbits appears to be a basic form
Of motion right down to the minutest
Quarks that are said to be spinning and I

Take comfort in the speculation that
Time and being and consciousness are not
Linear with a definite and a
Final beginning and end but they are

Just like the setting and the rising sun
Reemerge and life will keep happening.

My quirky
personality
will not
continue
indefinably
but
consciousness
may.

We live within a spectrum of things but
What's really significant are the poles
Of opposites as the world appears to
Be either hot or cold and day or night

And right or left and alive or dead and
Hateful or loving and I can only
Know what summer is in reference to
Winter and can only experience

The wonderful knowledge of compassion
In opposition to indifference
So being also has its opposite
That is nonbeing and one involves the

Fullness of life but the other dissolves
To the absolute emptiness of things.

I cannot
even form
a conception
of the
absolute
absence.

He stopped eating yesterday which was a
Stark difference in his behavior as
He yowls at me incessantly until
I present him with food that compels me

To practice patience because losing my
Temper doesn't quiet him and makes me
Miserable while I appreciate
He's lived since my kids were in grade school and

Now they're grown and living apart from me
And through twenty years Johnnie was a calm
And affectionate cat it's true with quite
A voracious appetite but during

These hard years he's become so bedraggled
Diminishing slowly to skin and bones.

When I found him
lying lifeless
on the basement floor
I knew my home was changed
forever.

In the last years of his life Johnnie taught
Me about patience as he could only
Eat prescription food and he dwindled to
A frail and skinny cat incessantly

Yowling for food which was a burden I
Learned to bear as no matter how much I
Provided he kept on wasting away
And I could usually manage the

Noise and I always felt sympathy but
Occasionally he was way too much
And I found the limits of my patience
Getting angry and yelling at Johnnie

But even then he couldn't be quiet
And I could only keep feeding Johnnie.

I learned to
practice patience
with my
impatience.

When I was growing up I resisted
My Dad's dogmatic and dominating
Personality as he stood apart
From popular culture with vehement

Distaste for rock music and hippies which
Embarrassed my adolescent yearnings
And opposition to him prevented
My appreciation of his passion

For classical music but with hindsight
I perceive that his everyday engagement
With Schubert Mozart and Beethoven on
His cherished grand piano must have been

Among the happiest hours of his
Life when he could escape disharmony.

After all these years
I appreciate him
for demonstrating
how to harmonize.

So much of my childhood was a response
To my father's dominance forming a
Resistance and opposition to him
And of course I didn't understand that

Growing in such a manner only made
Him more dominant as he became the
Impetus of my reaction and in
Cosmic terms perhaps he was the Big Bang

And I've been expanding ever since but
In the interweaving of billions of
People whom I will never meet and of
Billions of events that I didn't cause

Each will have inescapable effects
In forming the nature of who I am.

I hope these poems
will have an
illuminating
and worthy effect
on my kids.

This is a poem about falling down
Which is something that happens to us all
Because we aren't as attentive or as
Graceful as we would like to be and the

Sequence is a slip coincident with
A quirky jerk followed by a moment
Of panic and discombobulation
Leading to the intense awakening

Of impact when all the elements of
Consciousness are concentrated at a
Single point of space and time which may be
Articulated variously from

Person to person but usually
I find myself ejaculating "ow!"

I don't know about you
but the embarrassing
blow to my ego is
worse than the
bruises.

My house where my family lived is not what
It was when it embodied my son and
Daughter and ex-wife and six felines as
Our kids are grown and gone and my former

Spouse is living elsewhere and five of our
Cats whom together we loved have died with
Johnnie departing just this week leading
Me to realize I no longer need to

Close my bedroom door to prevent him from
Entering and yowling before dawn and
Rousting me from my disembodied dreams
And I understand there is no longer

Any occasion within my house for
Me to keep the doors between the rooms closed.

There's no need
between Kitcat and I
to practice privacy.

Seldom can I gaze leisurely at the
Ascending sun without glancing aside
To prevent its blaze from damaging my
Eyes as this morning it appears as a

Mild orange disk without a corona
Similar to the harvest moon and the
Moon is only a harmless jewel of
The sky but this is the mighty sun the

Originator of life on earth shorn
Of its majesty and I realize
Ash in the atmosphere has drifted from
The wildfires in California across

The continent suffusing the air I'm
Breathing and dimming a cloudless morning.

After cooler days
we are having a
resurgence of warmth
but my breathing is
labored with smoke.

The world is always burning as the earth
Has a molten core with pressure building
To bursting with flame and ash and today
California is burning with wildfires

And the air is red with flame while smoke is
Diffusing in the atmosphere crossing
The continent subjecting the country
To a shower of ashy particles

And America is convulsed in a
Political season with a frenzy
Of accusation and dishonesty
Disorienting and dispiriting

Disinformation setting people off
Silently defensively violently.

In the interplay of
air water fire earth
the element of flame
dominates today.

Johnnie is gone now and I do miss him
But his absence is providing a more
Comprehensive understanding of Kit's
Personality and I think I've been

Mistaken by ascribing devious
Motives to Kit's deportment supposing
That he manipulates and bosses
Me about by caterwauling to be

Fed again immediately after
I've just fed him as now I'm recalling
A glimmer of a thought from years ago
That I forgot amidst harassment that

Kitcat has way too much energy and
He is very easily distracted.

Kitcat's not
manipulative
he's flighty.

As the shine of the sun is cresting the
Horizon I can see a mist rising
From the valley and disintegrating
In the crystal air while the prominent

Oak tree and the limbs of other trees in
Pioneer Park are black silhouettes and
Are extensions of the twilight and I
Am grateful to be wearing my winter

Jacket and hat and socks and gloves that are
Counterbalancing the sharp onset of
Cold autumn temperature but as the
Minutes pass the leaves acquire color

With sprinkles of orange red and yellow
And the dew is sparkling upon the grass.

How much longer can
our small gathering of
ex-drunks continue
meeting in Pioneer Park?

There comes a day every year when it's time
To cut and bag the leaves and stalks of the
Hostas and daylilies within my yard
Which I have considered a dreadful chore

But today I am resolved to do it
And my method is much better as I'm
Using a hedge trimmer and not a knife
But whether I suffer through the hours or

Gather enthusiasm will depend
On where my attention goes and today
Is cool and sunny while last year was cold
And wet and I'm not mourning a broken

Relationship as I was last year and
My puzzles today are stimulating.

Cutting and bagging
daylilies and hostas
resembles a ritual
of sowing and reaping
attitudes.

I do delude myself into thinking
That I can turn the necessity of
A repetitive and laborious
Chore into a meditative and an

Uplifting experience but when I
Am doing the actual work I have
To untangle an electric cord and
Strain my legs and buttocks by bending down

To use the hedge trimmer at ground level
And I have to make sure to put down and
Pick up the rake from a place that isn't
Underfoot and when I am attempting

To stuff the stalks and leaves into lawn bags
I have to adroitly open and stuff.

Nothing is more frustrating
Than attempting to stuff
prodigious handfuls
into a halfway-opened
lawn bag.

We ex-drunks reserve a spot on a wall
Where we gather for the display of the
"The Holy Words of Pithy Wisdom" and
First is an admonishment "turn ye off

Ye holy coffee pot" which reminds me
To be awake and another says "let
Go or be dragged" which urges me not to
Be so domineering and a final

Suggestion says "it won't happen like that"
Revealing to me that no matter how
Sure I am about the scenarios
I create in my head when the future

Actually arrives what happens will
Be quite different from what I expect.

Too often
my cogitation
resembles the
planting of
landmines.

I suppose it's a sin to waste space so
The carpenters installed a couple of
Cabinets just below and along the
Ceiling of my house right behind where my

Refrigerator is nestled and the
Cabinets remain empty because I'd
Have to use a stepladder to reach them
But I'm not the only person here and

When I hear a commotion that I am
Not making I assume that Kitcat is
Up to something and this morning there was
A repetitive and mysterious

Knocking which was Kitcat playing with a
Superfluous and unreachable door.

I have a cat within a
cabinet behind the top
of my refrigerator
within the kitchen
of my home.

This is a curious and assertive
Creature possessing eight squiggly limbs
And a bulbous head with clever eyes and
An inventive mind capable of the

Tricks of camouflage and of evasion
As its entire body is squishy
And it can squeeze itself through narrow gaps
To hide within a den that functions as

A sanctuary and it is also
Able to fluidly pounce on its prey
Smothering and biting with a beak and
Imparting venom but an observer

Would have to submerge and swim among the
Kelp forests and coral reefs of the sea.

Oceans naturally
inspire mystery and
people have mythologized
the elusive
octopus.

Oh happy white page you are my trusted
Companion and I can come to you when
I need to communicate and when I
Am bursting with a sudden urgency

To epitomize and articulate
An aspect of my life that I have not
Yet completely digested and I know
The act of engaging with you and of

Expressing the exact words and phrases
That do comport with my genuine and
Heartfelt experience is not something
That I can accomplish all by myself

Because I need another receptive
Entity to draw out my hidden core.

I imagine
many appreciative
faces happily
listening
to me.

Returning home from Hudson yesterday
Rounding a bend and descending a long
Stretch of the highway which I have traveled
Countless times I remembered yesterday

Our returning home from our family
Overland driving vacations rounding
The bend and descending the same stretch of
The road fifty years ago and from the

Back seat of my parents' sedan I could
See a spectacular view of a wide
Expanse of the glittering river but
Today the trees have risen up and the

Welcoming home sight of the river is
Blocked living only as a memory.

The pageantry of the
autumn leaves decade
after decade marks a
deepening expanse
of today.

I am grateful for my new friend who said
To me that I am beautiful because
No one has said that to me before and
She revealed her generosity and

Also the difficulty I have in
Accepting a heartfelt compliment as
Something about the burden of having
An unappeasable ego creates

A craving for approval but when the
Gift is freely given I respond with
A disbelieving hollowness and I
Am grateful for the hours before dawn

When the words that people say to me have
The opportunity to resonate.

I am grateful for
my hollowness where
generosity may
resonate.

The world is like the pulsation of the
Sounding of a temple bell resonant
In crests and troughs and like the vibration
Of the photons of light speeding from the

Sun and also like the orbit of the
Earth around the sun emanating the
Bloom of apple and cherry blossoms in
Spring and the parti-colored leaves in fall

And like the migration of birds in the
Spring and autumn as everything goes and
Comes again in an inexhaustible
Combustible pattern pulsating with

Life as bodies age and pass away and
Other bodies are born and carry on.

I am a drop of
consciousness
alive and one
with an ocean
of consciousness.

In my youth I admired the poets
Who wrote fluidly flowing syllables
Who with a few concisely chosen words
Were able to express the poignancy

And precariousness of living but
As much as I tried sitting at a desk
Ransacking my consciousness for hours
I couldn't assemble a line of words

Because I was stuck on a needle's point
Creating so much unnecessary
Pressure believing with caffeine and with
A tremendous spurt of exertion I

Could compel a masterful moment
Of inspiration and the words would come.

I hadn't learned to
play with words
and to act with
liberated
spontaneity.

I am a drop of consciousness awash
In an ocean of connection often
Making distinctions between myself and
My own circumstances and you and your

Circumstances thinking anyone in
My place should comport themselves as I do
Not realizing that we share the same
Rippling of thoughts and I may respond

More or less with cooperation or
Opposition but we share a pattern
Of possibility creating so
Many personalities not knowing

I couldn't be the person that I am
Unless you are the person that you are.

When I forget
distinctions and
comparisons
I am happier.

While driving home from Minneapolis
Attending to the speeding traffic on
The highway and being careful to be
In the right lanes leading to Stillwater

I kept returning to the sight of the
Harvest Moon sailing beyond the scattered
Shreds of the clouds — and the luminous disk
Possessed me as if it were a fixture

In the night as an ornament to hold
On to in the midst of fleeting chaos
Because I am moving so quickly now
Precariously balanced and wanting

Amidst the velocity and tension
To find the encouraging poise I need.

This morning I strained
my index fingers by
pulling the aging hardware
of double-paned windows
into place.

Solstices and equinoxes go by
Without my noticing because I don't
Follow the calendar so carefully
And I don't have the specialized knowledge

That my friend Jason the ecologist
Does and he can see the uniqueness of
Every season and year after year his
Understanding of nature is growing

While I love apple and cherry blossoms
In spring and parti-colored leaves in fall
Because these seasonal changes apart
From the contention of human drama

Are the embodiment of loveliness
So bright delicate and ephemeral.

Autumn follows spring
spring follows autumn
birth to ripeness
ripeness to birth.

It is a handy trick in politics
To accuse the opponent of lying
When the accusers themselves are lying
And the impact is exponential if

The news people and the politicians
Share a common enemy — and if the
Fodder of accusation rises from
An interweaving of bureaucracy

Composed of distorted and secretly
Guarded information that is proffered
To news reporters regardless of the
Violation of the law then the game

Can be played inexhaustibly because
The bureaucrats remain anonymous.

Distinguishing
what is true
what is a lie
is exhaustingly
tricky.

Jim talked about his regret for having
Smoked for forty years and how he wishes
He'd stopped long before because now parts of
His lungs are useless and sometimes he wakes

From sleep gasping for the next breath in a
Fit of panic yet somehow he makes it
To another day not wanting to see
The doctors because they keep finding things

That are wrong with him and they're really not
Able to help him but the inhaler
Flovent — expensive as it is — does bring
Relief and a truck-driving friend coming

From Mexico brings him the Flovent he
Needs as in Mexico it is dirt cheap.

The five of us
listening to Jim
found nothing
consoling to say.

I do know what gasping for breath is like
Because I've had asthma from childhood and
I recall an incident triggered by
Inhaling the hay dust within a barn

Believing I was going to die but what
Usually happens today is I
Forget to check how many puffs remain
Within my inhalers as the drug is

Draining and suddenly my lungs become
Constricted and for several weeks I
Struggle needing the medicated mist
Of a nebulizer to ease breathing —

I resume with life-giving inhalers
Resolved not to be forgetful again.

The preciousness
of easy breathing
is so easy to
forget.

It happens when I am in a rush and
Not attending carefully that I will
Grab or pull something and crack a nail which
Causes a nagging discomfort when I'm

Putting my fingers in a pocket and
Rubbing the cracked nail against anything
So I'm compelled again to clip and file
My fingernails which I've learned to enjoy

Taking the time as an oasis in
A busy day as I can leisurely
Give my attention to the simple task
Concentrating on creating rounded

Ends becoming a true paragon of
Comely tidiness at least for a while.

I can drum my
fingertips upon
my desk in a
reverie of
joy.

This is a splendid time of the year with
The brightness of the leaves in the mellow
Sunlight giving the days an air of a
Festival and now we are having an

Indian summer with a resurgence
Of warmer temperatures after days
Of frosty weather and I've reopened
My windows and turned the heater off and

Can lollygag about my house upon
The floorboards in the morning in bare feet
Which is a luxury reserved for the
Summer and this afternoon my bike and

I will pedal in the countryside to
Discover whether the swallows have left.

The onset of the cold
compelling a resort
to warmer socks in
the morning brings an
air of seriousness.

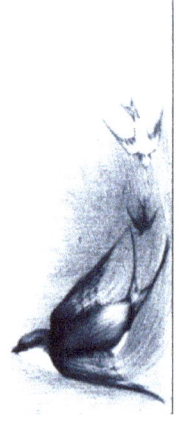

We are far enough along into fall
For the leaves to be accumulating
In the corners of the driveways and by
The curbs of the streets and the yellows and

Reds of the leaves are approaching such deep
Vividness it seems that the leaves themselves
Are radiating light and on a day
Without a cloud the sky is glorious

And contrasting with the silver pendant
Of the moon hanging weirdly within the
Morning sky as the sun is evoking
All the colors of the rainbow spectrum

And a scattering of single leaves are
Circling and wafting down to the ground.

Sun earth and moon
are perpetually
gracefully dancing
with each other.

On occasion I was a grumpy dad
More attentive to the busyness in
My head than to my kids and I recall
My Dad being elsewhere occupied too

Though I witnessed how he dealt with tension
Resurrecting Mozart and Beethoven
On his grand piano for an hour
After lunch every day but I disliked

The piano lessons practicing scales
Remembering only the metronome
Ticking off the time until my freedom
So without much consideration I've

Not imposed my enthusiasms on
My kids believing pressure doesn't work.

I am hoping
in the coming years
my kids will read these words
and remember me
with affection.

My mind is a bowl open to the sky
While I am sitting in Pioneer Park
For a meeting with my friends before dawn
As we are sitting in folding chairs and

Talking about duck hunting and plucking
Feathers and breasting the ducks and I don't
Understand what they mean as I'm alive
To the sounds of traffic emanating

From downtown Stillwater nestled within
Limestone bluffs as the geese are honking and
Flying and squirrels are about and a
Fringe of the clouds is pink from the sun that

Has not cleared the horizon yet but is
Already revealing autumn brilliance.

There is more to notice
than I am capable
of absorbing as the
moment continues
to ripple.

Of all the things to see while the leaves are
At their flowering of autumn color
My gaze is drawn to the silhouette of
My shadow speeding on my bicycle

As if I needed reminding that's me
Propelling myself along not sparing
A moment of ease even as I know
The image is only a symbol of

Who I think I am which is a paltry
Substitute for the kaleidoscopic
Panorama on display today but
By now I know it's better to laugh

At myself to relax and to
Play at racing to a liberation.

In the countryside
I have to be careful
not to smoosh dozens of
woolly bear caterpillars
creeping on the asphalt.

I've been initiated into the
Mystical vibrations of the chakras
And I'm excited to know more about the
Significance of the flowing touchpoints

Of energy manifesting in the
Spine especially because the perky
Woman who has lifted the veil of my
Ignorance is herself an enchantment

And she's discovered that my heart chakra
Is over productive and maybe new
Connections with her the earth and my
Rippling circumstances will dissolve the

Limited scope of my understanding
But now I have more questions than answers.

Does the
undulating
woolly bear caterpillar
have chakras?

The trees are quietly present through the
Years and seldom do they summon my gaze
Except with their vivid colors in fall
And afterward it's a shock to see them

Standing naked and beseeching the sun
With their upwardly reaching bare branches
And then they appear for many long months
Dormant and howling in the winter wind

And they are growing and aging at an
Imperceptible pace and they live and
Die like every living thing but as for
Me I am changing dramatically

Yet if I'm not carefully attending
I don't notice my metamorphosis.

The leaves are brightest
in spring and autumn
demarking incessant
transformation.

Sometimes it's fun to make the letters and
The words that I am sprinkling across an
Untainted page the objects of my love
Reminded as I am of the dropping

And doodling of Jackson Pollock without
Striving overmuch about the meaning
Of the words imagining as I am
That the letters are like the leaves swirling

In the wind with the shape of the letters
Corresponding to the species of the
Trees and with the flurry of syllables
Approximating the gusting of the

Breeze separating the turning leaves from
The trees without a ponderous meaning.

What is the meaning of
winter dormancy and
summer splendor besides
life continues?

This is my 50th poem and I'm
Keeping track on the way to 100
When I may congratulate myself for
Having completed another book as

I am measuring my worthiness by
The number of pages that I've written
Which is becoming like celebrating
The next birthday on the way to frailty

But then I can play with the idea
Of Jackson Pollock dribbling his paint
On an empty canvas and providing
Joy to so many people who are not

Likely to be bothering much about
The meaning of things beyond playfulness.

The weight of
contrived identity
may be dissolved
in playful expression.

I have been writing these poems with the
View that not many people would read them
Beyond a small number of my friends and
Thusly I've felt liberated to write

About risqué topics that I wouldn't
Want my mother to know about and when
She expressed an interest I continued
To feel secure in my secrets because

She's not familiar with poetry and
My poems aren't a page-turning novel
And I assumed she'd never discover
What happened upon page 505

Believing that every preceding page
Is an impeding veil of secrecy.

My presuppositions
are different now
but I'm pretty sure
she won't read this
poem on page
1551.

Before the dawn the valley was dark but
A wide expanse of the water was light
Reflecting an open stretch of the sky
And I was finding the chill in the breeze

Sharp but stimulating and I could see
Several miles downriver the pinpoint lights
Of red and green blinking on the bridge and
On a couple of the boats and slowly

The grainy bark and the remaining leaves
On the trees in the park were becoming
Visible then suddenly the red of
The sugar maple tree was glorious

As the clarity of daylight arrived
And I was happy to be a witness.

It's hard to explain
how exhilarating
it can be to lose
myself in simple
observation.

I've been working with a consultant for
The improvement of my publication
And he's a whiz-bang at conversation
Specializing in gibberish about

His detailed experience conveying
The impression that he's beneficial
But it's impossible to get him to
Focus on what he needs to do for me

As he is urging me to work harder
Even though he knows that I'm exhausted
As I'm sinking into the quicksand of
Reading another of his emails that

Proposes my immersion in a plan
I didn't ask for and isn't helpful.

Scrutinizing a
misbehaving
printing press is
much easier than
fixing people.

I exult within a luxury of
Sanctuary from whatever crazy-
Making agitation is consuming
The hurly-burly activity of

Business by coming to my computer
Letting my hands loiter upon my desk
Centering my chin upon my palm and
Rejoicing with the harmonious joy

Of morning composition selecting
Words transforming experience into
A pursuit for elusive moments of
Insight composing nonsensical lines

Of poetry and reforming trouble
Into a blaze of glittering whimsy.

I can churn and grind
my prevaricating
consultant into
a piquant
tomato paste.

The blades are sharp and ready
The gears and wheels are oiled
I crank the handle
Around and around
And the paste comes spurting out.

A frost arrived along with a forecast
Today for three to five inches of snow
While the yellow leaves are still clinging to
My cottonwood so I'm not able to

Dispose of the leaves before the onslaught
Of winter which for more than 20 years
Has demarcated the pivot of the
Seasons when with the dynamic motion

Of my body I rake and I gather
Handfuls of leaves and stuff them into the
Open lawn bags which is trickiest when
The bag is empty because the bag will

Stubbornly resist staying open and
Many of the leaves refuse to go in.

Little handfuls of leaves
using my left hand to stuff
and my right hand
to hold the bag open
obtains satisfaction.

It's odd to see so many leaves on the
Trees after the first snowfall showing an
Overlapping of seasons with sticky
Snow clinging to the branches of trees with

The dropping of the melting snow and the
Pooling of water within the lower
Places of the landscape and perhaps these
Chickadees hopping in the snow leaving

Tracks and darting their heads about haven't
Seen snow before but I am noticing
A milky overcast sky reminding
Me of uncounted winter days as much

A memory of my body as of
My mind's testimony of endurance.

Having uncollected leaves
scattered about my yard
underneath the snow
is a bothersome
untidiness.

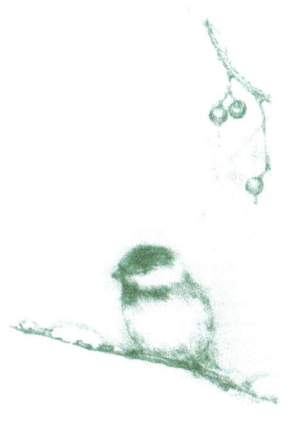

I dreamed about putting on my white snow
Boots again that reach up to just below
My knees and they retain some of their tread
And they are smeared with a grayish grime that

Resulted from my 23 years of
Clearing driveways enduring endless steps
Through crunchy sloshy salty grungy muck
And laces at their tops are serving to

Seal impermeable fabric about
My legs protecting my shin bones from the
Abominable chilling sensation
Of snow sliding all the way down to freeze

The most vulnerable part of me that
Goes stiff before anything else — my toes.

Apparently snow
penetrates my
psychic sanctum
though it doesn't
touch my toes.

They were not like the Honeycrisp apples
That are in the supermarkets and lacked
The crisp tastiness and fresh aroma
Of the highest quality but they were

The last remaining apples from the trees
That I planted in my yard twenty years
Ago and from July I have had the
Satisfaction of eating first the soft

Yellow apples of the one tree and then
The later ripening red apples of
The other but now with snow on the ground
Much earlier than expected I have

Emptied my refrigerator of my
Homegrown fruit and summer is consumed.

I keep forgetting
in the midst of
summer bustle
to pluck the fruit of
my raspberry bushes.

The sight of snow on the roofs of houses
Under a milk-white sky with a winter
Chill in the air that seems to arise from
The snow on the ground is a shock to a

Body even when my mind is busy
With political controversy as
A dampening quietude settles on
The land but this year the transition has

A surprising overlap as a maple
With flaming orange and a cottonwood
With cheerful yellow leaves haven't yet dropped
Their leaves and in my moment of morning

Awakening I am celebrating the
Flux of the symbols of the seasons.

Blue jays and cardinals
sprinkle winter days
with color but maple
and cottonwood leaves
usually don't.

I've gotten a confirmation from one of
My board members about my consultant
And our suspicious are correct — that he
Is having memory problems — and now

We know why he said one thing on Friday
And its opposite on Monday and why
He forgot appointments and belabors
Me with lengthy emails that are devoid

Of substance resolving me not talk
To him for fear that I would erupt with
Words that I would regret and what is to
Do otherwise than to surrender my

Wrath to feel sadness and to give him a
Release from expectations and duties.

A dampening quietude
not of companionship
but of responsibility
is only humane.

My memory resonates when I see
Gulls flying about Stillwater looking
Very much like the seagulls of decades
Ago wheeling in the gray skies about

The long seawall of Galveston Texas
Comporting very well with the ceaseless
Cresting of the waves of Galveston Bay
Where the poignant cries of the seagulls would

Reflect back to me the loneliness of
My self-imposed exile far from my friends
And family when I thought that I could
Find myself by running away but now

The gulls of Stillwater Minnesota
Remind me of youthful exploration.

Sights and sounds
pepper memory
with inspiration
with reverberation.

The sky is white today with a tinge of
Gray imposing an air of somberness
As if we have been overcome by the
Weightiness of winter in the passing

Of days as if someone had stretched a lid
Over the earth as a circumstance that
Cannot be reversed but I can see an
Intense sphere within the whiteness burning

And radiating the whiteness as a
Shining disk almost as painful to see
As looking at the sun in an open
Sky but now the radiance is serving

Only to gauge the height of the clouds and
To provide the clarity of daylight.

I sprinkle letters over
a white computer screen
tinged with gray as if
I were writing a poem
on a winter sky.

The abrupt transition into winter
Is most obviously noticeable
In the sudden starkness of bare branches
With leaves scattered everywhere on the earth

As the leaves are bereft of colorful
Vibrancy becoming dry and drab on
The ground and I am seeing the many
Denuded trees under an overcast sky

With every limb rising up beseeching
The nourishing radiance of a sun
That is withdrawing a measure of its
Potency which is a sobering fact

That there are barren seasons of life and
Perseverance is a necessity.

As winter drags
the novelty of
bare branches fades
and trees become
almost invisible.

A neighbor is burning leaves as I am
Driving by reminding me of childhood
Memories when the burning of leaves was
More often done and I am breathing in

The poignant aroma while the finest
Grains of snow are almost invisibly
Descending from a white sky full of a
Glowing daylight as the height of the sky

Is impossible to gauge as the sky
The light and the descending snow are one
Phenomenon as a crow is perching
On the topmost twig of an oak and I'm

Marveling that the twig can bear the weight
Of a crow who knows what the twig can do.

There is less color
than a week ago
but infinity
abounds.

I'd like to address you my reader with
Appreciation and offer a few
Words of explanation of what I am
Doing exploring this moment at my

Window creating a sanctuary
Of tranquility and allowing the
Sights and sounds that I've been absorbing like
The gulls that reminded me of seagulls

To resonate and I am hoping to
Inspire you to pause over the words
And to recognize the quiet within
Yourself so that the everyday sights that

You've been absorbing like an overcast
Sky may reverberate as metaphors.

This moment of
experience is the
imperishable point
of the spear
of now.

I close the curtains of my house in the
Evening before darkness arrives and when
I rise from sleep I roam about the rooms
Engulfed in the darkness before the dawn

As the nighttime of winter extends its
Wings further into daylight and I take
Comfort in the rushing of the furnace
Blowing warm air throughout my house and I

Enjoy the coziness of walking and
Sitting within the many islands of
The glowing electric light bulbs within
My home as it seems to me that the world

Outside is diminished and the inner
Realm of quiet and thought is magnified.

After all these years
I am more sensitive
and better aligned
with the rhythm
of the seasons.

I may align my energy with the
Sun cresting the horizon and lighting
The bare trees the sides and eaves of the homes
With the wispy clouds drifting south and it's

Easy to be optimistic when day
Is breaking with a vibrant sky and I'm
Here to witness the few moments when the
Angle of the rising sun touches the

Trees with light and then the light diffuses
Leaving the silhouettes of the starkly
Bare trees brown under a transforming sky
As the pace of the clouds is gradual

And the daylight is ordinary but
The clarity of morning is joyful.

Morning clarity
is often followed by
conundrums
nagging details
evening dullness.

I hated having my round boot laces
Come undone as I was pacing about
Stillwater because I'd have to stop and
Stoop over when I'm in a hurry and

When it's cold outside I don't want to take
Off my mittens exposing my fingers
And the ordeal is embarrassing
In the midst of strangers but thankfully

I've been educated about double-
Knotting my laces and it works even
With round boot laces and it's easy to
Take the floppy rabbit ears and twist them

Round again and now I'm liberated
Bounding about unhindered and happy.

The problem with
ignorance is
I'm unaware of it.

I like to read in bed before going
To sleep with my eyelids wavering and
Drowsiness getting the better of me
With an elbow and palm propping up my

Head when the lazy flop of a tail strikes
My face as I didn't notice but here
He is sprawling strategically beside
Me seizing my attention with an act

Of brazen audacity not once but
Repeatedly looping and lashing me
With the tip of his tail flickering as
An explanation point of sassiness

And what could I do otherwise than to
Rouse myself and snatch his face with my hand.

With one hand I seize
his face and let go
with the other I slap
his tummy and Kitcat can't
defend both at once.

If I slept as much as he does I would
Be a pathetic slouching excuse of
A human being and he doesn't do
A useful thing lounging as he does in

A spot of sun or near the duct from the
Furnace where warm air is blowing and he
Gazes at my boisterous busyness
With fluttering eyelids on the verge of

Sleeping but now and then he'll sit upright
Furiously biting a spot of fur on
His tummy or scratching behind his ear
With his rear paw because apparently

He is assailed with itches and I
Think it's great that he is doing something.

But if I attend
too much to him
I find myself
assailed with
itches.

I need to replenish the water in
The aquarium as a portion has
Evaporated and I can hear the
Continuous pouring of the water

Into the tank and reverberating
And I am neglectful when it comes to
Doing things that aren't immediately
Necessary however now I am

Noticing the liquid loveliness of
The pouring of water that resembles
The flowing of a creek over stones in
A secluded wood which is a peaceful

Sensation much better than its absence
Whispering consistently in my ear.

Does the pitter-patter
of poetry approach
the musical quality
of pouring water?

My daughter took wedding vows dressed in a
Kimono in the presence of seven
Of us inside an art gallery by
Addressing her beloved with these words

That she loves his laugh lines and his shaved dots
His warm eyes and his youthful heart and the
Ignorant jokes he makes and even when
She is groaning she loves him as they have

Together painted murals and fled the
Pope kept an animal alive survived
A quarantine moved across the country
From the sands of the Jersey Shore to the

Stone-scattered coast of Lake Superior
Coalescing elements into one.

Together their
days are richer
laughter deeper
hearts lighter.

I arrived at my Mom's house yesterday
To drive her to my daughter's wedding and
As expected she was 15 minutes
Late in getting ready and I soon got

Over that and the ceremony went
Well and I was happy she got to see
Her granddaughter's marriage and this morning
I noticed that the sun visor with the

Mirror on the passenger's side was pulled
Down so apparently during the trip
She took a sneaky peek in the mirror
To check her appearance which is what my

Ex-wife did and also what a girl that
I take to poetry readings does.

Being male
I don't need
a mirror festooned
onto my
sun visor.

When I listened to a recording of
An enlightened master propounding the
Dharma by reciting poetry I
Compared my verses with those that he chose

And concluded that there is too much of
Me in my poetry as the verses
He employed were broad and impersonal
And perfect for his intention and I

Was downhearted but after a while I
Considered I can't be otherwise than
Who I am at the moment poised for
The opening insights that come my way

Enraptured so often by glimpses of
The unexplainable joy in trifles.

Is it not remarkable
that every being
has lived with the same
sun moon clouds
and roses?

Today is unexpectedly warmer
And on the afternoon of Halloween
I am able to ride my bicycle
On the circuit where weeks before the leaves

Were bright to see so much of the color
Is drained away with the corn and soybean
Harvested with stubble stalks and stems where
The wildflowers were and the crickets

Are silent and so much of what was green
Is brown with interspersed piles of snow and
The river is rippling and reflecting
The gray of swiftly moving clouds and yet

The wind is bracing but not icy and
My pedaling is exhilarating.

There is an
austere and lovely
harmony to be
savored.

I keep the stone I found in summer on
My desk absentmindedly turning it
Until its curves are fitting perfectly
Within my palm with my fingers folded

Over it realizing its size and
Shape wouldn't comport with just anyone
As the holding and turning and smelling
Of it is comforting as my mind is

Elsewhere but now I'm wondering how it
Came to be whether it was subjected
To crushing pressure smoothed and rounded by
Eons of flowing water and whether

It was one with the molten rock of the
Lifeless ages billions of years ago.

It's not a homeless
asteroid as the
forces of the earth
are shaping it
today.

I saw it while driving on Halloween
Not knowing the significance of it
And I always appreciate the sight
Of a full luminous moon in the night

Because it reminds me of the ancient
Chinese poets who wrote about the same
Moon a thousand years ago but today
My friends remarked that it was a blue moon

Which doesn't mean as I supposed that the
Moon looks blue but that because it seldom
Happens that a full moon will appear twice
Within a single calendar month so

When the lucky coincidence occurs
We have a catchphrase to celebrate it.

The moon shone in the west
as the sun rose in the east
this morning equally
welcome.

I'm mindful of a message I've received
To love everyone and to tell the truth
Yet the truth is I don't love everyone
And most of every day I give myself

To politics which is about power
And manipulation and people who
Accuse their opponents of committing
The very crimes that they are guilty of

Which creates confusion and bitterness
And endless tribal animosity
And to put even a toe into the
Quicksand of the daily controversy

Is to become immersed in the loathing
And the dread of victorious tyrants.

I know too much about
the rules for radicals
and the manipulation
of mass consciousness
to be complacent.

So today my loving everyone and
Telling the truth will become my *koan*
As today is election day and the
Culmination of a spiteful season

Of politics coinciding with the
Return of warm and beautiful days when
I may take the opportunity to
Rake the fallen cottonwood leaves and to

Stuff them into lawn bags and maybe the
Gathering of the leaves will resemble
The counting of every vote or perhaps
Simple activity will liberate

My melodramatic predicament
And I may relearn to laugh and let go.

You can't really
forget or ignore
or conquer an
authentic
koan.

Because of the early snowfall and the
Chill afterwards I thought that I would miss
My autumn ritual of raking the
Leaves which would spur an awareness of an

Additional chore to be done in spring
Which would nag my consciousness throughout the
Winter even though I would be blameless
But the unexpected reappearance

Of an Indian summer with such mild
Temperatures has cleared the way for me
To take the very simple task in hand
That every year the cottonwood will drop

Its yellow leaves and overcome the ground
And I will summon the will to bag them.

The leaves drop in
different places from
year to year and the
pattern of my thoughts
will vary.

A blue sky in November is without
The blazing brilliance of the summer sun
And when I close my eyes and face the sun
I cannot detect its throbbing presence

But even though the impetus to growth
That raises fruit and vegetables is
Somewhat drained and the quality of the
Light is becoming increasingly bleak

I believe the light of the winter sun
Is precious beyond price as if the sky
Were like a diamond and with a correct
Angle I can see the light refracted

Into all the colors of the rainbow
Because the air and the earth are precious.

A crack in the glass
of a window has revealed
to me the rainbow colors
hiding inside of
winter sunlight.

We have a tradition in November
To turn our clocks an hour backward and
Favor the sunrise over the sunset
And on the morning of the pivot the

Difference was like magic as at once
There was much more of the daylight and
With the shocking reappearance this year
Of Indian summer I was able

To gather and bag my leaves into the
Afternoon wearing a T-shirt and shorts
Which is beyond my experience in
November and it almost seems as if

This is an extraordinary year and
Winter will not come to Minnesota.

I can see the
squirrels
everywhere
frisky in
bare branches.

The pandemic virus has been active
Around the world for perhaps a year and
In America and in Stillwater
We've minimized our contact person to

Person while the presence of the airborne
Virus is forcing people to wear masks
Inside stores and schools and public places
Placing a persisting strain on people

Isolating and exacerbating
The divisions of a nation that was
Volatile before the pandemic and
After the presidential election

Halves of the nation do loathe each other
Portending endless bitterness ahead.

People who are
recovering from
alcoholism and
drug additions are
hard put to be sober.

Half a dozen of my friends and I are
Gathering in Pioneer Park for the
Conversation that our sobriety
Depends on at 7 am resolved

To meet throughout the winter on Monday
And Friday and we are bringing our chairs
A container for a fire and winter
Clothing and this will be an endeavor

To tell our grandchildren meeting in the
Dark before the dawn watching the sunrise
With clarity arising over the
River valley conversing and thereby

Adjusting our attitudes sharing
Openness willingness and honesty.

We look forward to
turning our will and lives
over to a power
greater than ourselves
for strength and guidance.

The oak in Pioneer Park reminds me
Of the distinguishing form of all the
Oaks with its limbs extending in such a
Peculiar and angular beauty and

This morning a large crow is cawing in
The oak sending and receiving cryptic
Messages in the neighborhood until
It flies away as the sun is cresting

The horizon in a sky clear of clouds
And suddenly there are two suns with one
Arising in the rippling waters of
The St. Croix River as I am hearing

The words of my friends in between the sights
And sounds of the park mixing happiness.

Staying sober
growing toward
lighter attitudes
mixes purpose and
unexpected joy.

What is a plinth between friends as I know
Sometimes you tend to go wobbly and to
Droop from one side to another as it
Is tricky to be balanced everyday

So I assure you that I will be here
As your weighty substance bearing you up
Immovable in a topsy-turvy
Environment where beings of beauty

Delicacy ornamentation and
Of ethereal quality need to
Be firmly held and undergirded
So I reassure you I will be here

When the gravity of the earth threatens
To topple you I will become your plinth.

My dear are you one
who doesn't bother with
dictionaries and instead
guesses at the meanings of
words?

No one was to blame when my family
Moved from Hutchinson Kansas to Bayport
Minnesota when I was nine years old
Because my dad got a better job and

I didn't recognize the impact of
Losing my first genuine friend who lived
In the house on the other side of the
Alley longer back than my memory

Can fathom and I don't remember what
We did together after more than five
Decades but there came a day when I did
Realize that the grief of losing my

First friend is alive in me today and
That the way I do friendships was altered.

I trusted Eric
completely and
disappointment
loneliness and
hurt arrived
afterward.

He is almost thirty years old and is
Making his decisions returning to
College to add an accounting degree
To the engineering degree that he

Already has while living in Juneau
Alaska far away from where he had
His childhood growing in surprising ways
Being smart and independent and an

Overnight manager of a deli
Often much too busy to talk to me
On the phone and I'd love to discover
How he arrived to where he is from where

He was but perhaps he himself doesn't
Know beyond the fact that he had to go.

Joshua my son
Jocelyn my daughter
are seizing control
making decisions
navigating the world.

She says when I talk about discordant
Topics or mention a person that I've
Been entangled with that she notices
That I depart from my body meaning

That a passion takes me and I am
Not calmly present but agitated
My breath is labored and shallow which is
A fact that I can verify and her

Words direct me inward asking what I'm
Noticing and often I'm groping for
Answers sensing vibration along my
Spine watching my breath becoming deeper

Longer as she's revealing to me how
Thought and energy are interwoven.

Charkas
instantly
reflect
a shifting
thought.

Temperate and beautiful days are rare
In November so I seized upon the
Opportunity to pedal with and
Against the wind on my bicycle in

My short-sleeved jersey descending into
Stillwater relaxed and cruising as a
Couple of teenagers are cavorting
On my left and one of them launches a

A skateboard directly into my path
Toppling me over the handlebars and
I roll without injury besides the
Blow to my ego and in my shock I

Swear as they apologize profusely
And I discover my bike doesn't work.

My bicycle season is
over as I walk my bike
up the hill to home
as the cold returns
tomorrow.

I was reading the creation myth and
Saga of Middle Earth by Tolkien when
I noticed a yowling commotion and
A cracking in the living room that drove

Me to investigate to observe that
Kitcat had fallen from his perch at the
Open window and he broke an ornate
Porcelain Chinese planter and he was

Agitated and responded to my
Questions by sinking his nails into my
Thigh which I didn't appreciate so
Much but what could I do otherwise than

Evaluate the fractures employ a
Roll of clear tape and repair the damage.

Whatever turmoil Kitcat
digested didn't last long
as he lounged on my bed
before lights out
as usual.

I do meditation before dawn for
The bliss of it and afterward I don't
Easily lose my composure but it
Happens after I've expended two days

Raking and bagging leaves expecting that
The Waste Management guys would come with their
Lumbering truck to toss the bags inside
And be gone with the dratted detritus

Of autumn so when they do not arrive
On the appointed day the gradual
Arising of anxiety with a
Touch of righteous anger tends to take me

Over so I call customer service
And wait on hold expecting an answer.

A pleasant woman
scheduled a courtesy
pick up for today but
now I'm worried whether
they will come.

In Aldi's the inexpensive grocery
Store I'm drawn to the coffee section by
A hypnotizing splash of glossy bags
Of brown orange red and blue reminding

Me of Christmas ornaments and I choose
The light roast ones because they provide the
Most rousing dose of caffeine and their names
Are enticing delicious and tasty

Of Hazelnut of French Vanilla and
Of Morning Brew and the bags aren't very
Big and they don't last much more than a week
But they grace me with the presumptuous air

Of being an unappreciated
Gourmet who finds himself lost at Aldi's.

I open the bag
by pinching and pulling with
thumbs and index fingers
and smell heavenly
Hazelnut aroma.

I settle myself on my cushion in
My living room in the dark with a straight
Back with my legs crossed eager to wash the
Weightiness of preoccupation from

My mind and I start the timer on my
Smartphone and hear the resonant ringing
Of a bell three times and the energy
Begins to flow but then I remember

I forgot to push the button on the
Coffeemaker and smoldering I
Unfold and rise to do the deed before
Resuming the posture and reminding

Myself forgetfulness is a blessing
If I don't worry too much about it.

Percolating bubbling
coffee filling my house
with rippling sound
and aroma is
fetching.

Coffee is a boost on any morning
As welcome and as enlivening as
The sun rising and I can't imagine
Not spooning the non-sugar sweetener

And not pouring coffee into my two
Containers before leaving home holding
Weighty containers while locking the door
Heaving the garage door up and getting

Into my car while handling the coffee
Sometimes relying on the crook of an
Elbow so when arriving at my desk
And window I may summon a glimpse of

Insight and prod my intuition and
Sip a burst of clarity and ponder.

On any morning coffee
is a boost especially
with overcast winter
gloom.

By the time I'm in the bathroom after
Preparing coffee cleaning the litter
Box feeding and watering Kitcat the
Drowsiness of sleep is gone and I am

Washing my face with watery warmth as
The tips of my fingers are splayed about
My face rubbing and splashing with soapy
Enthusiasm knowing as I do

Now is the time for the percolating
Of thought as my stream of consciousness is
Supple and spontaneous as I'm not
Attempting to manage my mind but I

Am letting it go wherever it will
And it's a pleasure just to cogitate.

Drawing the razor
over my cheeks and chin
swiping away shaving cream
from under my nose I am
clarifying life.

I keep the 50-pound dumbbells under
The light table and out of the way for
Convenience after I've exhausted my
Head with poetry and bodily I

Prepare for a shock positioning them
Wide apart as elevated grips for
Pushups or in front of a chair for curls
Resolved to overcome the revulsion

Beforehand exerting utmost effort
Expanding labored breathing heart pounding
Blood pumping the veins about my temples
Throbbing gasping for air near finishing

Counting repetitions but I struggle
And sometimes I am just not accurate.

Apprehension
beforehand
dissipates
into
satisfaction.

The gray of the sky is overbearing
The nakedness of trees is foreboding
Seven inches of snow are forecasted
And winter swallowed Indian summer

But I am not worried about my lawn bags
Because they have been collected and the
Rituals of autumn are now complete
And there's nothing to do but wait for snow

The roads and the sidewalks will be icy
The blizzards will come continuously
The city snowplows will be sweeping piles
Of compacted snow across my driveway

And I will do what I have always done —
Put on my big boots and shovel stoutly.

Seven crows were
stabbing the carcass
of a car-smooshed
rabbit across
the street.

An overcast sky
like the whiteness
of an empty page is
pregnant with
possibility.

—*Tekkan*

Everyday Mind XVII

The drizzle falling
slantwise in the wind
yesterday froze
onto my driveway
and sidewalk overnight.

We don't want to go inside because the
Virus is most contagious within rooms
And meeting online by video is
Not as good as person to person so

On Monday and Friday at about dawn
We ex-drinkers and addicts gather in
Pioneer Park on a limestone bluff with
A view of the wide and winding river

Southward and with downtown Stillwater
Beneath us and we can see the sun rise
The Crossing Bridge 3 miles in the distance
And the steel frame of the Lift Bridge below

As the few of us warm ourselves around
A fire in a portable container.

We each take a turn
we don't interrupt
we talk about being
free from addiction
and the joy of living.

Because yesterday was my 63rd
Birthday Darlene and I shared a cake and
She sang the birthday song and remarked how
Happy to be starting my 64th

Year which dampened my spirits because I
Was expecting that I would be having
Every month for 12 months the enjoyment
Of being 63 years old but no

Said Darlene who is better with numbers
As she patiently explained that at birth
We are 0 years old for 12 months and
Then we have our first birthday and begin

Living our second year which is very
Clarifying but also depressing.

I am older than
I thought I was
but not as smart.

What is the benefit of writing with
10-syllable lines making sure in the
Process that there aren't any extra words
Or phrases while being careful to be

Clear in meaning and to choose the exact
Word for a worthy idea because
I can't say that all of this falderol
Will produce better poetry or will

Elucidate the world more profoundly
Or poignantly than other poets do
But I excuse myself by saying that
I like playing the game that I'm playing

Am having a dump truck load of fun and
Poetry keeps me away from squabbles.

1 at a time
chickadees come
to the hedge outside
the window hopping
and darting away.

I have leveraged the uplifting joy
Of natural beauty to balance the
Dreary business of watching politics
Enclosing the squabbling human drama

Within the vibrations of the cosmos
But hatred and polarization are
Gaining momentum and the news is now
Political and it's increasingly

Difficult to trust the worthiness of
Media and I am frightened by the
Prospects of dictatorship confronting
Insurgency while I am determined

To find a sustaining poise transforming
Wrenching chaos into enlightenment.

A flock of birds
flew and settled into
high cottonwood branches —
a squirrel jumped
from the trunk to a branch.

Due to a spike in infection rates of
The pandemic virus and the sudden
Stress on hospitals doctors and nurses
The governor is closing restaurants

Schools and gyms again leaving me nowhere
To go for exercise in winter so
I bought a stationary bike in a
Box at Walmart and unpacked it in the

Living room and misassembled its parts
For several hours because instructions
Are usually boring and somehow
I managed to bolt everything backward

And upside-down making for myself a
Metal statuary of abstract art.

After exhausting
every mistaken
configuration
I persevered and
a bike has bloomed.

Before I bought the stationary bike
I thought economically and bought
A $3 jump rope and rolled up a
Portion of the rug in my living room

And learned that what was so easy 40
Years ago is not the same anymore
As my calf muscles and shins are not as
Springy with the 20 additional

Pounds to lift and even though in summer
I can race up the hill to Houlton on
My bicycle I realize today
That imitating the butterfly bounce

Of Muhammad Ali is a fancy
Better reserved for another lifetime.

The cycling motion
of the stationary bike
doesn't impact
my knees
and ankles.

The word from the governor is that gyms
Will be closed for a month but I believe
The closure will last much longer because
That is the pattern of pandemic and

Mandate so I went online to buy a
100-pound cast-iron dumbbell for
Use in my living room allowing me
To lift 100 times without stopping

With my back and left hand and then with
My right hand and I won't need the gym and
I'm saying goodbye to the gym where I've
Gone for 15 years and goodbye to my

Friends and I will miss our banter and
With whom will I complain about the news?

David owns the gym and
he's worked so hard and
renovated everything
and now maybe he'll
lose his business.

I don't believe anyone is to blame
As each of us brought opinions to the
Practice but I found myself leaving our
Saturday morning meetings upset and

Alienated and during the week
Before the next meeting I watched myself
Preparing verbal ammunition and
Arguing in my head and opposing

The most dominant figure in the group
And this pattern of agitation grew
Over years and is contrary to how
I want to practice meditation on

The way to waking up so I'm thinking
It's time to make a change of direction.

I am saying goodbye
to the group for now
surrendering arguments
seeking harmony
meditating.

I am aware that my profession of
Political commentary on 1
Level complicates my Buddhist practice
But on another I believe there is

A harmony to be discovered but
Recently I've watched as an entire
Network of national broadcast news has
Altered its ideology slowly

And now suddenly which is a scary
Consolidation of the replacement
Of balanced reporting with agenda
And propaganda news and I am sad

It's not possible for me to trust the
People I've listened to for many years.

How do I assimilate
watching shifting
balances of power
while pursuing
liberation?

I can see the many ways the world is
Evanescing into difference in
The ripping out of the road on the way
To the post office and in the paving

Of new asphalt and in the altercations
Of politics and the way those who I
Know talk about politics and in the
Way my friends and I aren't able to be

Friends in the nurturing way that once we
Were but it's more difficult to see the
Many ways that I am evanescing
Into difference as I am building

Defenses and seeking for other ways
In which nurturance is obtainable.

Anger is easy to see but
it's more difficult
to accept
grief and sadness.

In November the rain may plink and plunk
Upon the earth and then the air may freeze
And the rain becomes a dribble plunging
And spattering onto the windshields of

Cars and onto the streets and the walkways
And the drizzle stings the skin and sticks to
Concrete and asphalt making walking and
Driving slippery and dangerous and

Then the spittle may become the snow that
Doesn't have a predictable pattern
As it may blow sideways in a bitter
Wind or it may meander down gently

Circling in the tiniest of snowflakes
Caressing my face with teeny kisses.

If I didn't have to
move the snow from
driveways and
walkways maybe
I would like it.

In April Jason and I walked in a
State park and Jason bounds at a great pace
And we walked for a long distance over
Several days and on the morning after

The first day I discovered 3 of my
Toenails were black because my shoes were too
Tight and pinched which I ignored because I'm
Stubborn and they looked bad and I thought that

They would fall off but they didn't showing
Me that I don't know much about how the
Body operates as it decides
What to do without asking about my

Opinion so for 7 months I've been
Watching anticipating a result.

Funny ridges emerged
where the pristine growth
is pushing out and
I'm trimming off
the black nails.

There are many things to be heard in the
Hours before dawn when the distance is
Alive with vibrations and I did not
Notice it until suddenly I did

And could not determine from whence it came
As it emerged as a constant rumble
Weighty and throbbing in my ears and I
Realized that it was freight engine

Pulling quite a long train of cars in the
Country conforming to a schedule and
Proceeding to a destination and
Rolling deliberately over rails

Doing prosaic duty in the night
Mingling its rhythm with quiet darkness.

The quiet darkness
is pregnant with
life and
possibility.

I don't always feel at home in the world
And if I may make an analogy
I would compare myself to a fish who
Doesn't belong to any school of fish

Who indeed enjoys exploring the depths
Of the river and savors the deepest
And mysterious bottom wallowing
In the muck and then I do like slinking

Within and without of the warm rays of
The summer sun near the upper portion
Of the world but I am solitary
And I don't like being solitary

And once I feel winter enclosing me
With an icy grip I just yearn to leave.

I rouse myself
for a mighty effort
a leap of faith
and jump
out of my skin.

My going out of the house every day
And to the office is nothing new and
I wouldn't know how to live otherwise
But for Kitcat who spends every moment

In the house my leaving and shutting the
Door is the resumption of solitude
A solitude not of his choosing but
Imposed upon him for which I feel a

Little guilty and I wonder what he
Does when I'm not home but this morning he
Stared and pounced and swiped at the overlarge
Rabbit ears I was making while tying

Bootlaces and double knotting as if
To say go ahead and leave you big dope.

Returning home
driving onto my driveway
unlocking and opening
my door I see him
at the door.

The view outside of the window from the
Desk where I watch the sunrise and compose
Poetry and edit a journal of
Opinion is the background scenery

Of my consciousness so much better than
Looking at highways and strip malls as I
Can see bare branches in winter and
Foliage in summer backyards and middle

Class homes and through the bare trees the other
Side of the river valley during the
Winter and there comes a red juvenile
Squirrel who runs along the top of the

White wooden fence within easy sight and
He peppers my days with a dash of red.

Whatever opinions or
passions emerge into
my consciousness
arise from this
homely scenery.

Today is Thanksgiving Day which is a
Worthy tradition in America
But it can be tricky eliciting
An obligation to be grateful which

When one is burdened with a self-imposed
Sense of solitary weariness can
Instead summon a twinge of grievance but
I have only to flip a switch in my

Head to recognize my girlfriend and a
Stationary bike and a 100-
Pound dumbbell paid for with my property
Tax refund and morning clarity with

A view of the river valley and a
Little red squirrel to feel gratitude.

I am really grateful
that grumpy
obsession is only
temporary.

During this time of tribulation when
We are compelled to keep distance between
Each other because of the pandemic
Virus we meet online by using an

App called go-to-meeting which enables
Us with streaming video to appear
On screen from the comfort of our houses
And Glenn projects his image while sitting

In his garage with large sheets of plastic
Spread and looming about him that looks to
Me especially in the gloomy light
Like he is plopped in the middle of a

Huge net of cobwebs implying that in
The dark a giant spider is lurking.

I've warned Glenn
a bite from such a
garage spider
is worse than
the virus.

Even nightime dullness is pleasantly
Relaxing because I'm not expecting
Of myself that I have to accomplish
Anything so that I can lounge in bed

Reading about Tolkien's Middle-earth but
Morning is my favorite time of day
Because I can experience my mind
Waking up and extending probing thoughts

And it's not as if I need to lift a
Shield and grip a sword to make things happen
But when I feel my energy surging
With the sunrise then naturally there

Comes a purposeful enthusiasm
And everything I do becomes easy.

In the morning
I could mince a
garage spider
with a sword
without even sweating.

A kitchen knife is not a sword but it
Is handy for cutting celery and
Mushrooms and oranges and cashews to
Go with the turkey breast simmering in

The slow cooker as I was functioning
As the chopper and following Darlene's
Directions immersing myself in the
Simple task of slicing an onion with

A better method than I had known and
The delicacy of mincing garlic
Excludes extraneous thought reducing
The entire cosmos to what happens

Between my fingers the garlic and
The busy blade making such tiny bits.

On Thanksgiving day
Darlene and I had
a mushroom side dish —
breading — turkey — cranberries
pumpkin pie — whipped cream.

There is no snow on the ground now as we
Have had such a crazy season of snow
And thawing but the trees are bare and their
Branches and twigs look to be scratching a

Blue sky this morning and I'd have to be
Nuts to get on my bicycle when the
Air is cold and I do think about it
But I've got a stationary bike in

The living room separated from the
Buffeting wind and the challenging sight
Of the great distance ahead of me that
I have chosen in summer to traverse

Expending energy in becoming
A fleet pedaling racing animal.

I pinch my bicycle
tire on the way to the
living room where I
pedal while listening
to music.

A candle's flame is combusting in a
Gentle flickering fascinating to
Focus on as a metaphor for the
Daily expenditure of a lifetime's

Energy surrounded by the darkness
Of uncertainty and a purposeless
Striving so taxing and wearing down of
One's spirit over difficulty and

Time and what is a candle's flame besides
Oxygen molecules breaking down and
Moving quickly and appearing as a
Wavy glow on a wick supported by

A cylinder of wax filling a dark
Room with a weirdly cheerful tiny fire?

A lifetime's energy
is a miraculous
opportunity to
discover what
is joyful.

I do personalize uncertainty
Extending my probing thinking outward
Beyond my skin touching the 10 thousand
Things I can't control and beyond to the

10 million things my imagination
Cannot even conceive of yet and in
My yearning I address my questions to
A God of my understanding composed

Of molecules and sunlight and wind in
Winter trees and circumstances and the
Troubles I can't see around the corners
To timely solutions yet and so I

Pray for strength and optimism not in
Words so much but in gentle persistence.

Everything coming
to me and everything
proceeding from me
is a baffling and seamless
happening.

I am not going to say it's "nuts" to ride
My bicycle outside in the winter
Even upon November 28
Because it was warm enough and I saw

That the deer lying dead by the road in
Autumn has become a skeleton and
That the pebbles I avoided since the
Summer have been thrust aside by snowplows

And that the sun in late afternoon was
In a different place when I went west
Over the Crossing Bridge glaring at me
And obscuring my vision and I could

See that the vast river was becalmed and
Reflecting empty sky and wooded banks.

Again snow
melted and maybe
winter will not come.

How forgetful I am and grateful to
Be forgetful because if I were so
Burdened as to remember everything
That has happened I'd be comparing and

Second-guessing all of my behavior
And calculating and how difficult
It would be to be spontaneous and
Free from care but of all the events that

I could remember I have the habit
Of holding on to the painful and frightful
Memories creating an edited
Version of the past and playing the role

Of an unlucky victim steering me
Forward to repeat some of my mistakes.

Am I choosing
subconsciously
what to remember
what to forget?

The questions arise who is doing the
Remembering and the forgetting as
The pattern of life is going on and
Is there really a solid someone as

Stubborn as the Red Spot on Jupiter
Spinning like a perpetual whirlwind
Or is the collection of memories
And predispositions apparent now

Only a cherished illusion as a
Someone who is afraid of engulfment
Abandonment and nonbeing who clings
To life and clings with a terrified grip

Perpetuating needless suffering
And who is dissolving and emerging?

Maybe that's what
liberation means —
getting out from
under
me.

These pages are a fabrication of
Paper and ink and glue combined with the
Watercolor paintings and the pencil
Drawings of my daughter's artwork and the

Images and letters are presented
By computers and the books are formed by
A corporation relying on the
Internet for whatever profit may

Result and every book is assigned a
Number in a catalogue managed by
The Library of Congress recording
The efforts of millions of authors of

Billions of words each of whom propagates
A germ of the madness of a culture.

Our books are
like bubbles
compared with
Egyptian
hieroglyphics.

It is civilized to page through a book
To have the curiosity and peace
To absorb the harvest of a writer
And sit in a chair giving up the time

That could have been productive by doing
Something else so I am saying thank you
To anyone who happens on these words
And am disclosing that the methods I

Use were pioneered by Japanese and
British poets and today I'm making
A little joke as I am offering
You the everyday appeal of the hedge

Outside the window where chickadees are
Are stopping by hopping and saying hello.

I see the chickadee
the chickadee
sees me without
falderol.

The steel garage door was difficult to
Lift today and the wheels were in place and
The wire cables were OK but it took
Me a dozen heaves before I could make

It rise as if there were nothing wrong with
It and it wasn't jerky which to me means
That it doesn't need lubrication so
I'm at a loss to explain it other

Than to suppose that mechanical things
Behave strangely when suddenly the air
Plunges much colder than freezing as I
Can see steam rising from the chimneys of

Homes and a hoary frost is on the ground and
The folds of my jeans are cold and painful.

The sensations of
sudden bitter cold
are inevitable
in Minnesota.

The little squirrel runs along the top
Of the fence and the top of the fence curves
Up and down between the bigger posts that
Make the fence's framework so the little

Red squirrel runs up and down on the top
Of the fence and then it turns the corner
And it keeps running up and down and out
Of sight behind a shed and then a bird

Perhaps a sparrow flies to the topmost
Branches of a maple and perches for
A moment and then it flies away as
A time emerges when nothing happens

Until the squirrel is running up and
Down along the top of the fence again.

The white fence
outside my window
down a little hill
seems to be
important.

It is always the same sun exerting
A supremacy on the upward swing
Hypnotizing us with an illusion
Even though Copernicus revealed that

The earth is rotating on its axis at
1,000 miles an hour and the ground
Under our feet is moving and it takes
Me an effort to remember how much

Differently this same sun would appear
Rising over the Sahara blasting
The air burning the sand and compelling
Every living thing to adapt to its

Might as the sun smolders variously
Depending upon its proximity.

Trillions and trillions
of unseen suns
are swallowed
by vast
darkness.

The delivery on the sidewalk of
My 100-pound dumbbell presented
A chore as it was enclosed in cardboard
Without an easy grip so I lifted

It by prying my arms under and heaved
Up with my back and legs and plodded up
Onto the 2 concrete steps with a strain
And opened the doorknob with a twist of

A hand and a wrist swearing because of
The damn pandemic that made its online
Purchase necessary but I recalled
That the dumbbell is meant to uplift my

Spirit through exercise and that I should
Be ecstatic to get it off the ground.

The cast iron
instrument
sits on the
living room floor
with aplomb.

How much easier it is using a
Tough strip of cloth wrapping around a wrist
And the handle while bending at the hips
With a hand planted upon the coffee

Table to raise the dumbbell off the floor
And lift it rhythmically as often
As I can as the dumbbell and I are
Like a pair of synchronized swimmers with

Me pulling one direction my partner
Precisely the opposite without a
Smidgen of a gap coordinating
Without an instant's hesitation or

Perhaps we are performing a duet
Of muscular music and gravity.

Heaving a weight
isn't really a
form of art
it's an ordeal.

Driving on the way to the post office
I saw by the street in front of a house
Upon a tiny bit of grass between
The sidewalk and the house a flock of pink

Flamingos newly placed there on display
For the residents of Stillwater and
I marveled at the pluck of the owners
Who most certainly know that people think

The birds are crass and hideous and these
Are not the ordinary plastic things
But they are tastefully constructed in
Blocky fashion of either metal or

Wood a half-dozen of them perched within
A little spot looking quite exotic.

The flamingos constitute
the owner's personal
Declaration of
Independence.

I returned home for lunch and met Kitcat
At the door and I bustled about the
Rooms and didn't attend to Kitcat but
I saw him pawing insistently at

The closed curtains in my bedroom so I
Opened the curtains and the bright sunlight
Spilled into my bedroom and onto the
Comforter on my bed brightening and

Warming the room immediately and
Instantaneously Kitcat flopped on
The comforter with an attitude of
Supreme triumph stretching outward with his

Fore- and hindlegs extending his long spine
And then he relaxed in satisfaction.

With a brain the
size of a walnut
Kitcat is good at
manipulating me.

Kit and I communicate outside of
The bounds of organized language within
A range of emotive exclamations
Of grunts and woofs and I will employ a

Rising inflection for indicating
Questions and we have a working routine
Going in the morning after I rise
From bed when I will grab a metal-toothed

Brush and Kit will trot to the rug and flop
And I move him facing away from me
And brush vigorously and sometimes he
Will twist and seize the brush from me and

Manipulate the brush turning the brush
Upward on the rug and will comb his face.

Holding it with his paws
Kitcat moves his face
across the metal teeth
studiously.

I've been writing a lot of poetry
Lately because doing my business and
Attending to and commenting about
The news has been awful lately filling

Me with disappointment as the people
I used to trust are no longer worthy
Of trust as I am opposing what is
Happening in the world of people as

The narratives emanating from the
Studios and newsrooms are becoming
Increasingly intolerant of the
Opinions opposing their own as I

Believe the various media shills
Are establishing an Official View.

Writing about
a little red squirrel
a 100-pound dumbbell
and pink flamingos
is much easier.

We are sitting in lawn chairs circling the
Container of fire with only half of
The moon looming in the western sky and
With the sun clearing the horizon in

The east and I am attending to the
Conversation about living without
Alcohol but I'm also watching the
Ceaseless harmony of the orbs from the

Vantage of Pioneer Park seeing that
A half of the moon is invisible
Because the earth is blocking the sun from
Lighting it as daylight is brightening

All the unnumbered branches of the trees
And the bare branches are glowing orange.

Living without
alcohol helps me
get out from under
the stridency
of thinking.

There are newcomers to sobriety
Who are talking about relapse into
Alcoholism and the lying and
The desperation that go along with

A return to addicted drinking and
I am grateful to have them reminding
Me of the hangovers and the haze of
Mind that didn't lift till afternoon and

Each of us has the opportunity
Of becoming truly liberated
Bringing us together for more than the
Genuine comradery because

We want to practice principles and be
Honest and willing and open-minded.

I could be in bed
with a headache
instead of watching
the sun the moon
and bare branches.

I am wearing the same shirts over again
Washing them on occasion to remove
The coffee stains and to luxuriate
In the freshness of clean clothes and I am

Shaving because I do reveal my face
To people without a mask once in a
While in person and more often online
By video but the colder temps and

The separation of people due to
The ongoing pandemic is weighty
Pushing me to grumpy ruminations
While shut within my home putting me on

Guard against the emergence within me
Of a resurrected Neanderthal.

Isolation
encourages
uncivilized
masculine
tendencies.

I remember from the earliest years
Being allured and captivated by
The nurturing and the gentle grace of
The feminine other and there were dreams

Of surprising adolescent stiffness
And release under covers during the
Night but I learned not to talk about the
Imaginative attractions bursting

Upon me and I was hesitant and
Hindered by the low opinion that I
Already formed about myself serving
To magnify and exalt womanly

Beauty stimulating excitement and
Yearning but also filling me with doubt.

I was burdened
with secret lust
and obvious
awkwardness.

My adolescent inhibitions are
Mostly a thing of the past and I am
Much more comfortable and civilized in
Conversation with the opposite sex

In abiding by the societal
Boundaries in my observance of the
Courtesies of companionship and I
Am skillful in listening and happy

To learn from Darlene to chop onions to
Brown beef with a little coconut oil
And to make tacos but there is also a
Certain awareness that in relations

Between the genders at least in my case
Women will always have the upper hand.

I have about me
an irremediable
cloddishness and
a tinge of the
Neanderthal.

Besides playing with words I am also
Using a cryptic saying of Zen that
Is passed down through the centuries about
A question from a monk and an answer

By a master — what is the way of Zen? —
Your everyday mind is the way — which sounds
Quite simple but becomes tricky with the
Method being to study the self to

Forget the self and thusly to throw off
Body and mind and be enlightened by
The myriad things because I am moved
To have liberation from suffering

But the masters also say that force of
Will or cleverness cannot seize the goal.

I practice
intention
patience
awareness
daily.

Meditation helps to clear my mind and
Listening to recordings of Alan
Watts provides helpful signposts on the way
As I'm attending to the glimpses of

Insight contained within what the birds are
Doing and how the moon the sun and the
Earth are dancing together and how good
It feels to cut vegetables for a meal

With the intention of being clear in
My perceptions and accurate in my
Selection of words and nevertheless
Knowing that how I think the world works is

Quite different from how it does work and
The best that I can do is be playful.

The best I can do
is to skillfully
tame or leverage
agitation.

I just love listening to Alan Watts
Who calls himself a philosophical
Entertainer with the idea I
Suppose that one might as well have fun with

Ineffable conundrums as words
Are incapable of conveying the
Authentic insight — and the traditions
Of Zen are beside the point but the point

Is to be discovered either in 3
Seconds or in 30 years — and neither
In earnest effort nor in purposeful
Carelessness can the point be realized

But once a person is infected with
The germ of the *dharma* it's hard to quit.

How do you get
to where you
want to go when
you have already
arrived?

My 100-pound dumbbell squats on the
Floor in front of the couch and under the
Edge of the coffee table where it is
Out of the way and when I am watching

TV and wearing socks I like resting
A foot upon the gargantuan hunk
Of metal because it is a brutish
Thing over which I have total control

Within my sphere of domesticity
And I fancy myself a heroic
Big-game hunter lording over his prey
Except that the dumbbell is still alive

So twice a week I put on my wrist wraps
Hunker down and give the weight a trashing.

After we are done
taking only minutes
my body aches and
I put it on the floor
with satisfaction.

My sturdy metal stationary bike
Is also held within my living room
Positioned toward a window and just in
Front of the studio piano and

Waiting and appearing to me like a
Gazelle on the savanna and when I
Mount the beast for my daily indulgence
I picture myself a crouching lion

Pedaling at a precipitous pace
Listening to music on my headphones
Elevated 4 feet above the floor
At chest level and I'm regretting the

Scenery as I did like to watch the
Girls pass by my pedaling in the gym.

A joking engineer
manufactured
road reflectors
on the pedals of
a stationary bike.

I notice that when I am standing up
My eyes are always looking at the world
From exactly the same height no matter
Which direction I am looking though I

Do have boots with exceedingly high soles
And heels that transform my perspective and
When I am sitting or lying down the
World towers above me just so much as

The length of height that I've surrendered but
Most everyone is taller than me so
When I am squinting up at them they are
Gazing down upon me however if

We were standing together on the verge
Of the Grand Canyon it wouldn't matter.

It is about time
to return to the
optometrist
because I am not
seeing as I did.

Of all the perks of writing perhaps the
Most peculiar and addicting is the
Glimpse of insight that piques my interest and
Summons my curiosity which then

Compels a lust for articulation
Because the initial insight is a
Tasting of the original world that
Comes because I am poised to receive it

And because there are unnumbered angles
From which to approach any subject the
Playing with syllables and cadences
And ideas and words is a game without

End which is truly joyous even if the
The product amounts to total nonsense.

I have no
idea
today what
I will write
about
tomorrow.

It sometimes happens that a poem will
Have a tail that extends to another
Poem and I believe I've underplayed
The magic of the original world

Making it seem as though I myself were
The dynamo conjuring creation
Which isn't true and I more resemble
A sentient bubble on the way to

Bursting and the multidimensional
Vibrations carry on regardless of
My attitude as every second I
Question with sight and sound and taste and touch

And smell and the world answers precisely
With sight and sound and taste and touch and smell.

And persistent thought
meets its opposite
a pregnant
nothingness.

While walking on the Crossing Bridge across
The river valley in autumn I gave
Up believing that in this lifetime I
Would have the opportunity to meet

A partner to share my life with and I
Accepted a solitary future
Because there appeared to be too many
Complexities in the way of finding

Compatibility and on the next
Day Darlene sent me an email from a
A dating app that I forgot thinking
That no one would want to meet during the

Pandemic but I was mistaken and
Darlene and I are happy together.

Having an inside view
on another person's
life dissolves many
limiting
perspectives.

Sometimes waves of energetic thinking
Keep me simmering at 3 a.m. and
This morning I remembered the pivot
In my children's lives when they left our home

And began fending for themselves leaving
Me the duty of surrendering to
Them their birth certificates and Social
Security cards which I remembered

Obtaining for them at the consulate
In Osaka Japan where I arrived
By train and subway from Kyoto where
They were born and I ruminated at

Night would they be able to keep them safe
Because those documents can't be replaced?

Sometimes
the nagging
details of life
persist beyond
usefulness.

When nervous energy keeps me awake
At 3 a.m. I am not attending
To what is happening at the moment
But I am tangled in a net of thought

Either regretting the past or fearing
The future when I'd rather be sleeping
And I would be sleeping except that it's
Difficult sometimes to relax and let

Go of the urge to manhandle results
But eventually I do let go
Of trying to control everything as
It's a simple fact that I can't so the

Question arises how graceful can I
Be being patient with my impatience?

Letting go of thought
trusting beyond
appearances everything
is OK is a subtle
practice.

I'm looking at the back-cover photo
Of Cid Corman's thin book of poetry
AND THE WORD from which Cid is gazing at
Me looking to be in his 50s which

Is much younger than my memory of
Him from 30 years ago in Kyoto
With an elbow propped on a desk with a
Hand holding his bald head with sad humor

In his eyes and with a pensive smile and
Behind him are unorganized stacks of
Books reminding me of my own boxes
Of books and when perusing his sparsely

Worded poems again I recognize
His slowly articulated anguish.

Cid loved
words
seizing
whatever
meaning
he
could.

When they have something needing to be said
They use facial expressions opening
Their eyes wide or positioning their ears
And when their ears are flattened back it's clear

There is trouble about and then they may
Bark or bray or snort or huff or even
Bare teeth as they are social animals
Meandering in the treeless grasslands

Or the woodlands or southward upon the
Mountains moving in herds and keeping watch
For predators and when in danger they
May run in zigzag fashion or a male

May lower his head and outstretch his neck
Prepared to bite or turn around and kick.

Is the
zebra
white with
black stripes
or black
with white
stripes?

Their skin is grayish or muddy brown but
Underneath they are pink being rotund
And weighty with long barrel-shaped bodies
Culminating behind with a tufted

Little tail to go with tiny round ears
However their heads are gargantuan
And they are social animals living
Together in rivers and lakes and swamps

Able to hold their breath underwater
For 5 minutes wallowing in water
Most of the day communicating with
Wheezes and snorts and grumbles and booms and

Mostly they eat grass and fruit but they are
Extremely volatile and dangerous.

With little legs overland
a hippopotamus
can chase a human
as fast as 30
miles an hour.

They eat crustaceans and birds and frogs and
Fish and locusts not like anybody
Else because they can't chew or break apart
Smaller pieces of food so instead they

Swallow whole whatever they seize and they
Ingest small stones to help with grinding food
Within their stomachs and because of their
Slow metabolism they will live for

Months without eating a morsel which is
Comparable with what Hindu masters
Will do but unlike Hindus in colder
Months or during droughts they dig burrows in

The sides of riverbanks and clamber in
And hibernate or maybe meditate.

Crocodiles have
personalities like
agents of the
Internal Revenue
Service.

They have the largest eyes of any land
Animal and they each have 3 stomachs
And their legs are laughably skinny but
They sprint 43 miles an hour and

Run 31 miles an hour over
Distance while only having 2 toes on
Each of their 2 feet but running isn't
Their only defense as they can kill a

Lackadaisical lion with only
A single forward kick and their mating
Rituals are quite ritualized and
Synchronized with the male excitedly

Flapping alternative wings and with the
Female running circles around the male.

The flirty ostrich
reminds me of
John Travolta's
disco preening in
"Saturday Night Fever."

They spend most of their time underwater
Maneuvering for krill and squid and crab
Fleetly turning with stiff little flippers
And webbed feet having a thin layer of

Blubber and tightly packed oily feathers
For preserving warmth but upon the land
Their dignity is somewhat diminished
As they waddle and hop and run with their

Bodies bent forward and they toboggan
Sliding across the ice on their bellies
Pushing with their feet and for protection
And warmth they huddle into colonies

Of large and noisy anonymous mobs
As numerous as thousands or millions.

Penguins in mobs
remind me of reporters
at the annual
White House
Correspondents
Dinner.

These creatures possess the most sensitive
Organ of any mammal comprising
150,000 muscles and
Capable of picking up a peanut

And shelling it and blowing out the shell
And then maneuvering the nut to be
Eaten and the same organ can be used
As a straw or a snorkel and also these

Animals use the bottoms of their round
Flat feet to notice the low-frequency
Vibrations transmitted through the earth so
They can detect the slow rhythmic stomping

Of herds of fellow creatures 20 miles
Away and matriarchs govern the herds.

What a
marvel all
the abilities
of the elephant
are.

This animal is central to the health
Of the ecosystem as it keeps prey
From overconsuming vegetation
Thusly maintaining the balance of the

Streams and forests and even croplands and
Its tail is 3 feet long and provides poise
When making a sharp turn and this creature
Can swim long distances and its hind legs

Are longer than its front legs so it leaps
20 to 30 feet and it hunts deer
Wild boar buffalo antelope mostly
At night with vision 6 times better than

Human sight but it hunts successfully
Only once in 10 or 20 attempts.

The beneficent
tiger is best kept
at a respectful
distance.

Almost everyone thinks this animal
Is white but really its skin underneath
Is black and it is a marine mammal
Capable of swimming constantly for

Days paddling with large paws while holding
Its hind legs flat like a rudder and it
Has a prominent nose detecting prey
Over 3000 feet away and it

Spends half of its life hunting for bird's eggs
And seals and small mammals and even when
Possible vegetation but it is
Only successful in 2 percent of

Its efforts demonstrating it takes grit
To survive amidst the Arctic Ocean.

Polar bears
frolic in the
Arctic but not
in the Antarctic.

These birds have microscopic crystal-like
Formations in their feathers reflecting
Different wavelengths of light so that they
Shimmer like butterflies and hummingbirds

And when the male fans its tailfeathers they
Quiver emitting a low frequency
Vibration and depending on whether
The female is far or near the male may

Vary the sound by shaking different
Parts of the feathers and the female has
Sensors within her crest that are attuned
To receive the same frequency sent by

Humming male tailfeathers so that when he
Flickers his plumage he rattles her head.

The male is a peacock
the female a peahen
offspring peachicks
together they are
a bevy of peafowl.

It's a whimsical notion to propose
A network of consciousness within which
Every being sports a quality of
Awareness comporting with an array

Of abilities fitting hand in glove
With an environment and suppose that
We humans and each of us as nodes of
Consciousness have paid our dues by living

Multiple lifetimes as beings using
An eagle eye or a fish wiggle or
A butterfly flutter or a polar
Bear determination and suffering

Wolfish hunger monkey mind or bullish
Irascibility or a fly's death.

Have you never met
a predatory human
reminiscent of
a tick?

Humans make a pastime of stargazing
In the beginning watching stars without
Understanding the orbit of the earth
Around the sun and the rotation of

The earth on its axis but now we are
Sophisticated gauging the movements
Of planets within our solar system
Predicting that within days and upon

The longest night of the year the planets
Jupiter and Saturn even though they
Are hundreds of millions of miles apart
Will seem to converge in the south western

Sky near the horizon looking brilliant
And earning the name of the "Christmas Star."

It's been 800 years
from the Earth's view
since the conjunction
of Jupiter and Saturn
was so visible.

Sometimes I have wanted to be at an
Event that divergent circumstances
Prevented and then at other times I've
Been to meetings where I wished afterward

That I did not attend for example
There were years of writing groups taking place
With Cid Corman after I left Kyoto
Japan and came to America that

I missed and on the other hand I would
Rather not have met the BMW with
My Corolla in the smash accident
On a side street in Minneapolis

As so often it seems that I was where
I was but wasn't happy to be there.

While planets keep
appointed places
my movements
are unpredictable.

Cid would read poems from ancient China
From America from correspondence
Would talk about when a crippled poet
Embarrassed and brought to earth a prig of

A poet and would dwell on the hardships
Of people he knew of turnings and dead
Ends demonstrating that writing only
Works when it tells the truth and it has an

Impact as about his enuresis
The unconcealable smell of sleeping
Sitting in his own piss which wasn't the
Terror but was in fact comfort and warmth

But always he heard Mother cursing Dad
Alone in the night hearing that door slam.

Lying in bed
thinking about
Cid I also hear
that door slam.

Every other Sunday for several
Years Cid led a poetry workshop in
My living room 30 years ago and
I considered how dissimilar we

Appeared and I reacted against his
Unwarranted pessimism as I
Believed with a doubtful optimism
But I looked forward to his baritone

Rambling even his tough assessment of
My writing because he had a hungry
Sincerity and intimate knowledge
Of the centuries of poetry and

He turned his egoism into a
Unappeasable thirsting for meaning.

Today
Cid Corman
influences
the leverage
of my words.

This poem was found
on a folded piece of paper
with Cid's looping signature
inside a book of Cid's poetry:

**WORK
SHOP
TALK**

There is of course a
word — <u>the</u> word. Think — feel —
become exact — be

at the point of it
point — going in the
direction you go.

—Cid Corman

I've been playing with dreams lately trying
To summon the will at poignant moments
To rise from bed and turn on the lights to
Scrawl words upon paper as a record

To ponder later and during daylight
I've been musing whether my visions at
Night are the spark of my unconsciousness
Inflaming my subconsciousness in turn

Subliminally cooking my walking-
Around mentality or whether these
Terms of psychology are really just
The idle mumbo jumbo of a few

Creative cranks and that dreams are only
Vibrations on another frequency.

Even in my dreams
I discover myself
striving
dubiously.

I don't remember being nobody
And the word "nobody" is a trick
When used in deprecation of someone
Who is contriving to be somebody

And it's difficult to be accurate
When saying "nowhere" because everything
Is residing in a place relative
To somewhere else and even beyond the

Sky the galaxies have their neighborhoods
And perhaps the most paradoxical
Label of all is "nothing" because it
Negates everything that so clearly is

And there isn't anything that isn't
Busy doing something going somewhere.

But once I was
nobody
nowhere
in the middle of
nothing.

What a burden in adolescence to
Be inflicted with acne dreading to
Look in the mirror and spot a fresh bloom of
Pustules boils or blackheads overnight when

Blossoming into self-consciousness is
A gauntlet of self-criticism and
Doubt generating a compulsion of
Comparison with the fortunate youth

Who have confidence and enchanting skin
During the critical seasons when the
Opposite sex is so mysterious
And comely when looking attractive is

Paramount then to be mortified and
Exposed to gossiping competitors.

I sometimes
envied dogs
with
furry faces.

Among the first words a child learns is "no"
Which is an omnipotent word but when
Coming from a mother its meaning is
Leavened with love intending only the

Safekeeping of the child but as life was
Happening into adolescence and
Adulthood the inconvenient hardship
Of having to hear the word repeated

And of having to endure rejection
In all the ways that "no" is not spoken
But apparent how agonizing it
Was for me — for myself — to find my

Balance to accept denial as a
Direction and not as a negation.

Learning how
to relax and not
care too much
is tricky.

A few of us are continuing to
Meet even as the temperature is
Getting colder and the darkness of night
Is lengthening as the winter solstice

Is approaching and we are stubbornly
Gathering in Pioneer Park huddled
Around a fire in a portable
Container and we are not wearing the

Prescribed masks during this vile pandemic
Season trusting to luck to a prudent
Distance we are keeping from each other
Dedicated as we are watching the

Sunrise savoring our happy talk and
Braving the happenstance of a rogue sneeze.

We are rebellious
primitives who didn't
bother building
Stonehenge.

There are those few occasions when after
Meditating I discover that I'd
Forgotten to push the button on the
Coffeemaker and that somehow I had

Sat for 40 minutes oblivious
To the absence of the bubbling brew and
The delicious aroma coming from
The kitchen next to the living room that

I love so much that somehow after years
Of practicing mindful awareness that I
Didn't manage what was most important
And that then belatedly I have to

Push the button afterwards and dawdle
Because I can't leave home without coffee.

I wonder whether
the Buddha was
ever impatiently
forgetful or if it's
just me.

I wonder what wry attitude someone
Would adopt looking at the life I am
Living which I myself believe is 1
Of burdensome complexity when what

They would observe is my useless sitting
On a cushion every morning followed
By my dawdling over poetry for
The most creative hour of the day

After which I deign to squeeze in a bit
Of work which is the only thing I'm paid
For — commenting on the news — and then there's
Lunch with "talk radio" and then a bit

More work in the afternoon leading up
To a lusty session of exercise.

It is an
impractical
solid-as-a-bubble
odd assortment
of doings.

It's a weighty question whether to put
Faith in linear time with a defined
Beginning and an uncompromising
Ending followed by an eternity

Of an uncertain locality or
Whether to allow oneself to be caught
Up in the swirl of cyclical timing
Comporting with the orbits of planets

The seasons of the year and the circles
Of the galaxies and the questions may
Be asked are the galaxies quickening
In a straight line away from the Big Bang

To lose energy and to dissipate
And then may the Big Bang happen again?

Is the questioning
remembering
forgetting person
a bubble that keeps
popping and bubbling?

Since I have made such a big deal about
Saying everything is busy doing
Something and going somewhere a person
May ask — what does a rock do? — and I say

A rock is lying on the ground or in
The ground and it is also moving in
4 directions at the same time with the
Earth rotating on its axis and with

The earth orbiting the sun and with the
Solar system orbiting the Milky
Way and even the Milky Way as a
Spiraling assemblage of a mob of

100 thousand million stars is in
A stupendous hurry going somewhere.

The Milky Way is
zipping 1.3 million
miles an hour to
who knows where?

On behalf of the livelier beings
Of the earth I would like to express my
Gratitude for rocks for the quiet and
The underlying and unacknowledged

Support that the rocks are providing us
Everyday in their variety as
Granite gabbro basalt limestone marble
Slate and shale in their evolution as

Igneous rocks that are molten and then
Cool as metamorphic rocks that are formed
By persisting heat and pressure and as
Sedimentary rocks that are scattered

Pieces of other rocks that are moved by
The wind water ice and biology.

Every pebble and
grain of sand has a
pedigree
originating
in mystery.

It wasn't immediately clear to
Me that 1 day I would appreciate
The taste of a dill pickle because in
My initial experience I do

Remember only its astringency
Compelling me to stretch my face in a
Kind of grimace and shut my eyes as an
Involuntary act of a futile

Avoidance so opposite was its tang
From say vanilla ice cream but don't ask
How my attitude changed or even why
I ventured another bite but doing

So brought me to an eventual point
Of admiration for its sharp appeal.

Maybe a clever
inventor is working
on a salmon
or a trout
ice cream?

I put it inside my mouth
and tasted it with my tongue
I contorted my face
And wrinkled my nose
The damage already done.

It is the Christmas season for giving
Gifts and for imagining what those who
Are on my list would find joy in maybe
A Star Wars or a Lord of the Rings thing

Comporting with particular passions
Or perhaps it's better to give useful
Gifts like kitchen knives or French berets for
Minnesota blizzards but this year I

Have propelled through the post office missiles
Of a strange and dubious quality
Inside of envelopes comprising a
Book of poetry written by me that

May be incomprehensibly dull to
Those who don't covet my odd obsessions.

Sometimes books
only serve to hold
other books upright
on shelves gathering
dust.

Jason told me the winter solstice passed
This morning at 4 a.m. which was a
Surprise as I had thought it would happen
Tomorrow and this morning the sky is

A gloomy gray and the landscape is a
Drab mixture of bare branches and lifeless
Grass without a covering of snow which
Is not typical and less cheery for

The season but I'm happy because there
Will be more daylight and less darkness from
Today and I am jaunty because I'm
Part of the vast cycle of the seasons

Accepting a gloriously gloomy
Day with the sun resplendent behind clouds.

The convergence of
Jupiter and Saturn
in the south western sky
may pass unseen tonight
by Minnesotans.

On the evening of The Great Conjunction
When Jupiter and Saturn converge in
The south western sky that also happens
To coincide with the morning of the

Winter Solstice the frictionless motion
Of the planets of our solar system
May be aligning and diverging in
Ceaseless dances about the sun but in

Minnesota we stargazers are stuck
Waiting for the forecasted clearing of
The clouds which given the iffy nature
Of day-to-day meteorology may

Or may not occur any minute now
As I am waiting with my fingers crossed.

Apparently the
daily weather
is harder to gauge
than planetary
orbits.

I'm able to see electric Christmas
Lights outside of the window now but not
The south western sky where I may or may
Not see The Great Conjunction which hasn't

Happened so uniquely in 800
Years so I'll take the occasion now to
Tear myself away from writing about
Wonderment when I could instead be a

Witness to the event so I will drive
To Hardee's family restaurant to
Order some takeout sandwiches to tide
Me over for the week and determine

Whether the Great Event is visible
And to escape the bother of cooking.

If we were Martians
living on the arid plains
of Mars the evening
would be a
nonevent.

I got the sandwiches but the planets
Converged out of sight beyond a layer
Of clouds and while driving I noticed a
Tinge of congestion and then a touch of

The sniffles prompting a remembrance
Of the occasional cough this morning
In Pioneer Park precipitating
A twinge of apprehensive questioning

About whether I was facing a cold
Or COVID-19 but such tweaking of
Doom didn't keep me from the satisfied
Consumption of 2 sandwiches nor did

It hinder my phone conversation with
Darlene while I was lying on the couch.

But on rising from
the couch I went on a
tear of vertigo that
caused me to
trip about.

My situation last night was not a
Comedy of a tinge of vertigo
But a whack of wooziness which left me
Wondering what to do beyond sleeping

Anticipating accelerating
Deterioration of my condition
Including a fever and nausea
And disorientation and fatigue

And chills compelling a separation
From people and a cessation of work
Which are what so many people about
The globe are experiencing but I

Mostly feared a constriction of my breath
A not-funny-at-all suffocation.

But beyond
a tinkle of
lightheadedness
this morning
I'm OK.

It's an ongoing tradition in May
In Japan to write poetry about
Cherry blossoms as they are fetching and
Delicate blooms brightening all the parks

After a season of barrenness but
It's tricky after so many years of
Creativity to find something new
To say so in Minnesota and in

December I will celebrate with a
1-of-a-kind tree in Pioneer Park
Diminutive and humble compared with
The surrounding trees but as closely as

I look there's no indication of a
Hint of the coming of cherry blossoms.

Absent cherry blooms
are a hint of the
emptiness
producing
everything.

Cherry blooms after winter year after
Year remind me of the resurrection
Of loveliness and winter solstice pricks
My consciousness of brighter days coming

Though January and February
Are months of bitter cold and piercing wind
As blizzards blow across Minnesota
As icy roadways become dangerous

And once Christmas and New Year's Day are done
Winter resembles a weary trudge through
The tundra where the city snowplows and
A homeowner's snow blower are symbols

Of determined resistance and mittens
Knitted hats and boots are magnificent.

The corners at the
end of my driveway
will become heaped
with piles of snow
higher than me.

Yesterday evening the clouds disappeared
And Jason sent me a photo by way of
The Internet taken I suppose by
His smartphone of the unconverging of

Saturn and Jupiter which will happen
Gradually day by day and I saw
A speck of light which isn't the light of
The planets themselves but is a fleck of

Sunlight ricocheting off the planets
And back to earth captured by a smartphone
And transmitted by email and into
The jewels of my eyes and now I feel

A little guilty I didn't have the
Gumption to see the sight honestly.

What impresses
is the vast
enveloping
darkness
unveiled
every night.

I am listening to the vibrations
Inside of the ear canals while I am
Sitting in a chair hearing the pumping
Of the heart as a rhymical thumping

And feel blood throbbing in the veins of the
Arms and legs and I am taking part in
The inflow of air in the nostrils and
Swelling the lungs with oxygen holding

For a moment and then releasing and
Can focus an awareness inside of
Each of the pinkie toes and fingers to
Sense pulsation and can extrapolate

While typing that the nails of the fingers
Need trimming but maybe not the toenails.

The pulsation of sunlight
even on a cloudy day
merges with the
throbbing of the
heart.

At 11 a.m. I listen to
Talk radio tuning in with the news
And the personality I like is
Expert at political scheming and

At characterizing politicos
And like everyone else commenting on
Politics there's a wallop of disgust
And ridicule and the listeners and

The host are equally caught up in the
Mission of defeating the other side
And the hangover from the election
Makes us feel defeated and desperate

With an unhealthy dose of betrayal
That is hard to hear and hard to turn off.

Listening to
or reading the
news is an out-
of-the-body
experience.

I gave my 100-pound dumbbell a
Kick but it proved to be unmovable
Upon the floor and I'm not intending
To engage with it until tomorrow

As it becomes a weight in the back of
My mind a day before our mutual
Involvement and in between our sessions
Of exercise I do admire its

Simplicity and brutal symmetry
Resting on the floor of my living room
Looking like a dwarvish piece of modern
Art complementing the stationary

Bike giving the chamber of my man cave
An ambience of steel barbarity.

I keep it under the edge
of the coffee table
enough out of the way
so as not to stub a
toe in the dark.

The ground a couple days before Christmas
Is without snow but it is raining now
And soon this afternoon it will drizzle
And then begin to snow and as it descends

The temperature will plunge to bitter
Cold forcing me onto my toes waiting
To make a calculation whether I
Can move the heavy wet most difficult

Type of snow off of 2 driveways before
The wind turns icy and the cold becomes
Unbearable as we have been lucky
Up to now but there's no escaping the

Eventuality of confounding
Recurring enveloping Arctic slop.

Where do the
crows and the
chickadees
shelter?

Winter lies dormant for half of the year
In Minnesota and for much of this
Winter we've been blessed with little snow and
Mild temperatures but over many

Seasons of blizzards I've developed a
Yet unrecognized malady of Post-
Traumatic February Disorder
In which the snowfalls from November through

April merge in the mind of a person
Into 1 weary phenomenon of
Shovel snow blower and city snowplow
Repeatedly playing over again

Disturbing even nighttime repose with
Dreams of shovel snow blower and snowplow.

From November through April
the threat of February
is just below the surface
poised
to emerge.

There are stages in the passage of a
Blizzard that are not at all unpleasant
Like when the wind is howling and icy
And the snow is zipping sideways in the

Wind and nothing is visible outside
Of the window except the blowing snow
And the temperature has plunged below
0 when I have warm exuberant

Gratitude for owning a furnace in
The basement and for using the curtains
Of my windows and for my electric
Light bulbs enabling me to don a

Bathrobe to close the curtains to savor
The heat and to watch a nonsense movie.

Then the world outside
the window does not
exist and there is no
February.

A reckoning comes the morning after
When I step outside the door into the
Snow and gauge the depth of the ordeal
And yes the cold was bitter today so

I donned 2 knitted hats the moon boots the
Elephantine mittens and the quilted
Long underwear girding my body for
Battle but firstly I noticed the wind

Had blown the snow off of the roof so the
Snow rake wasn't necessary and
The drifting snow wasn't deep and because
The cold came suddenly the snow wasn't

Wet and heavy but was fluffy and my
Snow blower works at its best in the cold.

My driveway
wasn't difficult but
an obstacle loomed —
my mom's
snow blower.

I yanked on the cord to start the other
Snow blower for my Mom's driveway over
30 times on 4 separate tries with
No success and before it has helped to

Be patient and to try again later
But this time I gave up while thinking of
My brother-in-law because he is a
Magician with machines and maybe he

Can fix it even though this blower is
Cantankerous and is more than 20
Years old and works well after it starts but
Getting it started is much more than a

Secondary detail because nothing
Happens without a propitious yank.

I'm a wordy guy
who has gotten through
many winters by
merely yanking
on cords.

Fresh fallen snow
on the day of
Christmas Eve
does look
magnificent.

—*Tekkan*

Everyday Mind XVIII

A chill arises with
fresh fallen snow
felt in the folds
of my jeans making me
alert.

It's remarkable how much depends on
The artificial demarcation of
New Year's Day as we do regiment our
Accounting of taxable income with

The closing of December 31st
And the starting of January 1st
And everyone wants to have a party
Celebrating another New Year on

The journey to senility because
What could we do otherwise than to choose
Frivolity over melancholy
As we need to have a ceremony

For passing time because we are human
And are compulsive at measuring things.

Getting plastered drunk
on New Year's Eve
and sobering up on
New Year's Day is
what we do.

I assert my liberation to mark
The passage of seasons according to
My predilections and on the verge of
Another blizzard of necessity

I raise my perspective from the prospect
Of the dull continuing routine of
Shovel snow blower and city snowplow
To the horizon of distant April

When Arctic temperatures are finished
And gritty grime-encrusted heaps of snow
Are melted when the sparkle of the sun
Begins to grow the grass and bud the trees

And when the glowing cups of the tulips
Are blooming and radiating sunlight.

Tulips are
resurrected
in April splashing
a barren landscape
with brilliance.

Kitcat was flicking his tail under the
Closed bathroom door while I was shaving and
When I seized it he began swiping his
Paw beneath the door as I was busy

With the razor attending to my face
Reinforcing an idea of who
I am by gazing in the mirror and
Hypnotizing myself with my image

When I realized that Kitcat doesn't
Have a conception of what he looks like
And he turns his head when I show him his
Body in the mirror and he is free of

Obsessional and sophisticated
Self-regard and he is mischievous.

He is frolicsome
while I can't imagine
getting by without
peering in mirrors.

I'm used to watching the sun cresting the
Horizon from my desk through the window
And in summer I can shut my eyes and
Determine the exact location of

The sun by sensing its pulsating heat
While during winter the sky is often
Overcome with a layer of white clouds
Tinged with gray and usually the sun

Is hidden but yesterday afternoon
While driving amid the freshly fallen
Snow I saw within an overcast sky
A white blazing disk of sunlight shorn of

Summer prominence but emanating
Enough light to clarify everything.

A gleaming
disk in the sky
has enough blaze
to keep the world
alive.

I listen to recordings of Alan
Watts who was a beatnik guru as I'm
Driving to the post office or Aldi's
Grocery store and though Alan has died

Decades ago he is a companion
Entertaining and enlightening me
With the lore and *dharma* of the ancient
Indians Chinese and Japanese with

Eloquence witty and humorous in
A cultured British accent and I have
Greedily attended scrutinizing
Every word and phrasing while intending

To saturate my being with him and
I've also heard him absentmindedly.

All the familiar
streets and highways
in all the seasons
are mixed up
with Alan's words.

Alan doesn't the minimize the horrors
And complexities of life but he turns
The context around revealing that each
Of us is an imperishable node

Of a cosmos observing itself and
Partaking in every sight sound and
Taste and when I experience the range
Of emotions confounded discouraged

Satisfied or absentminded I am
A universe at a point of ceaseless
Becoming evolving and emerging
With fresh circumstances and if only

I could drop my victimized perspective
I would be liberated from the past.

I don't completely
understand Alan
but he inspires
irrepressible
intuitive joy.

At our meeting in Pioneer Park when
The air is 6 degrees Fahrenheit one
Of us says that she is happy to be
Up before dawn with each of us because

It's important on New Year's Day to start
The first morning of another year off
On the right footing as we could have been
Passed out in bed and sleeping off a drunk

But we are clear-headed and bright-eyed and
Exuberant around a cheery fire
In a portable container recounting
All our blessings energizing ourselves as

We are observing the darkness dissipate
On a cloudless day with fresh fallen snow.

The branches and twigs
of the broad and tall
bur oak in Pioneer Park
appear to be scratching
the open sky.

When opening my refrigerator
Door and retrieving a container I
Find a ripe plenitude of overlarge
Blueberries inside of a plastic box

That I did buy a couple days ago
Without noticing the quality of
The produce within a busy day while
I was attending to many details

Plopping bananas and oranges and
Milk within my cart and too harried to
Appreciate the bounty awaiting
My attention until this morning when

I exuberate gratefully over
Finding such elephantine blueberries.

Usually blueberries
coming all the way
from Chile in winter
are hard and
pea-sized.

I am also grateful this morning for
Running into my gym buddy Greg at
Walmart where he passed on the word that the
Gym has reopened but because of the

Ongoing pandemic and a mandate
From government everyone throughout the
Building at all times must be wearing a
Mask during even the most heart-pumping

And breathtaking vigorous exercise
Which would be such a drag and a drain but
Not for me because a month ago I
Spotted an inexpensive and sturdy

Stationary bike inside a box that
I fortuitously bought at Walmart.

I can get happily
sweaty every day
without wearing
a mask in my
living room.

I am grateful that the temperature
Is in the low 20s and I hope that
The air continues to be so because
The snowfalls are fluffy and the snow is

Easy to move when the snow blowers are
Prepared and are a snap to start in the
Colder weather but the fresh fallen snow
Is spoiled by urinating dogs grimed by

Salt-spewing snowplows and the everyday
Traffic and trodden on by the squirrels
And worst of all the integrity of
My cleared driveway is cluttered by the gunk

Of the collected snow in my wheel wells
When the disgusting glop falls from my car.

After so many winters
all the details of the
season are
indelible.

Henry David Thoreau remarked on the
Quiet desperation that people live
Within and I interpret his words
To mean a sense of isolation and

A disposition to keep emotions
And disharmony shut within a stream
Of private thought compounding over time
Till a separation between self and

Other seems unbridgeable perhaps not
Encompassing every aspect of life
And not hindering casual give and
take but so regarding the desperate

Desire for communication and a
Mutual understanding and for love.

I testify to a
numbness
concealing
grief and sadness
with anger.

Alan says a poet can talk about
Anything and he describes the Hindu
Myth of presenting existence on the
Human level as a game of hide and

Seek wherein the divine says to people
Get lost and so with disharmony and
Dissatisfaction we do get lost with
An underlying intuition that

There is a happy union to be found
Creating a dynamic below the
Level of conscious awareness seeking
For wholeness which is the divine in us

Camouflaged within a vulnerable
Ego questing for a liberation.

Is my skin a
barrier or a bridge
between me and the
world as everything seems
to get inside of me?

Imagine the pages of a book to
Assume the aspect of the moments of
A life in which there are continuous
Zaps of insight as they are the sparks of

The divine maybe not the encompassed
Union of liberation but of fire-
Flies of understanding and of bite-sized
Portions of recognition presenting

How joyful overlarge blueberries are
How zestful predawn conversation is
And how year after year winter blizzards
Make a pattern burdensome but also

Beautiful when described as cycle of
Dormancy and then of resurrection.

I assume
everyday
something
is worth
communicating.

Each poem of mine contains only a
Single period after I've reached a
Tentative just-for-today conclusion
Before which is a compendium of

Turning phrases creating a single
Run-on sentence and there's no reason or
Rhyme for writing sonnets the way I do
Except that it's fun to express in a

Package of verbiage something worthy of
Expression perhaps balancing meaning
Maybe in a daring experiment
To test whether I can spur a reader's

Curiosity to the end before
The words collapse into jabberwocky.

After a while
arbitrary
pattern
assumes
a compulsion.

There are the winter days of blue skies and
Sparkling snow when the sun lights millions of
Bitty crystals and the snow is fresh and
Yet untouched and the trees are posturing

Revealed in their millions of gesturing
Crooks and angles unsymmetrical and
Dominating the landscape and frosted
With a thinnest tinge of snow and branches

And twigs are crisscrossing the drifting of
Snow with wild shadows interspersing a
Blanketing of the snow with patterns of
Purest light and gray wherein the more I

Look the more I see near and far pinpoint
Brilliant jewels refracting rainbow sunlight.

Drab overcast days
metamorphize with
open skies
fresh fallen snow
crisp air.

I've been alerted over the phone by
My girlfriend who has expert medical
Knowledge that it's not the dust itself or
Even the dust mites that everyone is

Allergic to but it is the feces
Produced by the dust mites that causes the
Calamity and I didn't mention
The congestion within my lungs or the

Stuffiness in my nose but she could tell
And I wasn't even aware of my
Condition until she told me and the
Casual tone with which she spoke as she

Revealed the mite-sized menaces lurking
In my rooms was shockingly effective.

I simply had to
bring out paper towels
glass cleaner
a broom and a
vacuum cleaner.

Stretching upon my bed
I try to drain my head
I blow my nose
And close my eyes
But can't stop sneezing instead.

Perhaps the mix of sensations involved
In a sneeze surpasses description and
One or even a series of sneezes
While I am sitting in a Zen posture

Calm and alert and apart from others
Where sneezing is without consequence is
Not so awful but during a viral
Pandemic when liquid begins sloshing

Within my nasal cavity with an
Ominous tickle in the nose that brings
A sudden light-headed anxiety
In the company of people — then I

Know with a dreadful certainty that a
Sneeze is coming and it can't be stopped.

Do I take the mask off
or leave it on?

We have something that the ancient Chinese
Poets didn't when they looked at the moon
And made it a symbol of mystery
And untouchable beauty as we have

The Apollo rockets and the Lunar
Rover and we know that moon dust smells like
Burnt charcoal similar to ashes from
A fire and our astronauts have trodden

On the orb without a sky and planted
A flag within the abominable
And the eternal silence of the moon
And we have seen that the scarring on the

Surface is a testimony for a
Propensity of cosmic violence.

The moon remains
a beautiful symbol
of untouchable
emptiness which
the poets understood.

I used to think that to be up on the
News in America I had to read
The daily articles commentating
On current events but now I see that

The reports are a repetition of
Violence scandal and tragedy and
That most of the information gleaned is
Gossipy distorted and deceitful

And that to gain an understanding of
What's really happening I have to trust
A few commentators who have proven
To be trustworthy over many years

Because nobody is capable of
Telling only facts minus opinions.

The doings of
mass numbers of
people are almost
incomprehensible.

Dino Derby

This creature's body stretched 40 feet from
Snout to tail which is about the length of
A school bus — standing 12 feet and weighing
8 tons and its gargantuan jaws could

Crush a car and a stiff skull allowed it
To channel all its Herculean force
Into the muscles of a bite with 6
Tons of pressure with 60 serrated

Teeth 8 inches long to pierce and grip flesh
Throwing an animal into the air
And swallowing it whole and it plodded
Forward headfirst on two mighty legs but

It possessed two puny arms that may have
Been evolutionary leftovers.

A large portion of
of the brain of
Tyrannosaurus Rex
was devoted to smell
similar to house cats.

This dinosaur had an enormous skull
With a backward pointing frill extending
In length up to 7 feet which had a
Thin flap of skin that stretched over solid

Bone and perhaps the whole formation of
The skull served as a device to display
Sexual dominance as the frill would
Flush pink with many blood vessels in its

Skin and it was an herbivore about
The size of a cow with 2 pointy horns
And a horn on its nose and a parrot-
Like beak which could clip vegetation and

It could chew with a few hundred shearing
Teeth within replaceable rows of teeth.

In marshes and forests of
western North America
Triceratops may
have been food
for T-Rex.

The Sinclair Oil Corporation uses
This dinosaur as its logo and the
Post Office put its image on stamps and
It must have had a mighty heart and high

Blood pressure to pump blood all the way up
Its long neck and it took 10 years to reach
Adult size — stretching 72 feet
Long — standing 15 feet high at the hips —

Weighing 17 tons — living as long
As 100 years — laying 12-inch eggs —
And breathing through nostrils on the top of
Its head and it was an herbivore that

Ate lots of vegetation and swallowed
Stones to help digestion in its stomach.

Scientists argue over
its name but currently
this thunder lizard
is called the
Brontosaurus.

Paleontologists call its spiked tail
A "thagomizer" in special honor
Of a Far Side cartoon and because of
The row of upstanding plates along its

Back — and because moviemakers added a
Tyrannosaur bite — it incarnated
Cinematic magic as "Godzilla"
And it stretched 29 feet long and weighed

5 to 7 tons and stood 9 feet tall
And lived 75 to 100 years
And it was an herbivore with a brain
Mass comparable with a walnut quite

Equivalent in size to Kitcat's brain
And Kitcat regularly outsmarts me.

Stegosaurus lives
in the imagination
of movie makers
cartoonists and
paleontologists.

This creature was a winged lizard and its
Young were dubbed flaplings by our whimsical
Paleontologists and it was a
Carnivore eating small animals and

Fish with an elongated beak fringed with
90 razor-sharp teeth believed to be
Active during the day — living 10 to
25 years — weighing 2 to 10 pounds —

And about 3½ feet in length —
With a wingspan of 3½ feet —
Discovered in Bavaria almost
250 years ago — and it

Waddled about on the earth on back legs
And with fingers on pointed leather wings.

Pterodactyl is
pronounced with a
silent "P" and means
winged finger.

This was an armored dinosaur and was
Considered a "fused lizard" because of
The bony plates on its back which are dubbed
Scutes and osteoderms and it ambled

About on four legs around 6 miles an
Hour — eating foliage — living 70
To 80 years — weighing 2 to 8 tons —
Stretching 20 to 26 feet long —

And it is thought to have had a good sense
Of smell and on the end of its tail there
Was a walloping and a whacking club
Which it could swing forcefully enough to

Shatter the bones of the toothier brutes
Which is why it is called a living tank.

The carnivores
would have had to flip
Ankylosaurus
over to get at its
underbelly.

These dinosaurs were pack hunters and lost
Out in our time because their name is hard
To pronounce and they could only trot at
6 miles an hour but the Hollywood

Moviemakers seized upon the razor-
Sharp second toe large curving talon that
Could inflict huge gashing wounds and their bite
Was like an alligator's chomping with

60 sharp teeth and they were 11
Feet long and weighed 220 pounds
And stood about 3 feet at the hip and
Maybe they had feathers but they were not

So smart as to be able to turn door
Knobs as they are portrayed in the movies.

Deinonychus
is pronounced
dyn-NON-ik-us —
nowhere near as cool as
Velociraptor.

Velociraptors were about the size
Of small turkeys as long as 6.8
Feet from snout to tail — weighing 33
To 43 pounds — standing at about

1½ feet tall — and they could sprint
40 miles an hour and they could jump
As they hunted but they didn't hunt in
Packs as portrayed in movies and their snouts

Were long and narrow with serrated teeth
And they ran on two toes on each of two
Legs retracting a sickle talon on
Each foot and they had two arms and hands with

Three curving claws on each hand and they ate
Small amphibians reptiles and insects.

Velociraptors had
Feathers — and raptor
means robber and
Velociraptor means
swift thief.

This animal was one of the largest
To roam the earth being 69 to
75 feet long — 15 feet high at
The hips — weighing 18 to 25

Tons and scientists debate about the
Flexibility of its 40-foot
Neck arguing whether it could lift its
Neck to eat the foliage at the top of

The tree canopy but they are certain
That it could swing and snap its 50-foot
Tail like a bullwhip terrorizing its
Foes producing a sonic crack like a

Cannon blast but now the snapping sound is
Gone and we can only imagine it.

Western North America
150 million
years ago was the scene
of Apatosaurus'
whipping crack.

In one of the "Jurassic Park" movies
A Spinosaurus has a slashing and
Toothy engagement with a T-Rex and
Snaps the T-Rex's neck and though it is

True the Spinosaurus is larger and
Has a cool-looking sail upon its back
Paleontologists observe that its
Jaws were not as mighty and its teeth were

Much smaller than T-Rex's teeth and yet
Spinosaurus did have a cruel set of
Claws 6 to 8 inches long capable
Of inflicting deep gashes but most of

The experts conclude Spinosaurus was
No match for T-Rex's terrible jaws.

The two creatures
lived at different
times and places —
Spino in North Africa
T-Rex in North America.

Since we have been unearthing their remains
We have given so much energetic
Imagination to recreating
Life as the dinosaurs must have lived it

Millions of years ago expending our
Fancy and speculation but I can't
Imagine the dinosaurs brainstorming
About us and figuring out what kind

Of animals we would be — so what kind
Of bizarre and otherworldly beings
Will be digging up our bones and fussing
Over us and puzzling about the fine

Details of our capabilities and
Will they discover our stupidity?

We live in a cosmos
of trillions of
galaxies beyond
anyone's
imagination.

What would it be like to be afraid that
The doctors don't care about you and that
The vaccine for the pandemic virus
Isn't intended to save but to kill

You because you are black and you aren't on
The priority list and also to
Be sure that the police are dangerous
And that the justice system is crooked

And to be surrounded by people who
Are thinking the same way reinforcing
A terrified isolated state of
Mind only somewhat relieved by reading

The Holy Bible that speaks about what
Is happening around you on this day?

The world seems
quite different
from various points
and I can't say
she is wrong.

After we started by reading aloud
From a book about letting go of the
Troubles of yesterday and tomorrow
And of fighting the battles of just one

Day — today — because anyone can face
The difficulties of just one day it
Is healthy to keep my mouth shut and
To listen as everyone takes a turn

In the circle speaking about what is
Going on today because I see how
Differently each of us is thinking
And how I create burdens for myself

Because I tend to believe what I think
And it is good to practice listening.

My thoughts may
become an endless
labyrinth but by
listening I find
today.

The pandemic is keeping people from
Mixing in light-hearted ways and a fear
Of infection is putting the entire
Country on edge as each of us knows of

Someone who caught the virus and there
Are deaths but life is continuing with
The stipulation that we keep 6 feet
Between each other in businesses and

In stores while wearing masks for whatever
Debatable good they do but most of
My sustaining communication is
Done face to face among a handful of

People and the words that we exchange are
Precious moments of camaraderie.

Messages coming over
computer screens
televisions
and videos
foster paranoia.

My moments of camaraderie give
Me the grace to see beyond my fears and
Frustrations to the cosmic mysteries
Wherein our political contretemps

And our pandemic virus are only
Storms fitting entirely within the
The drama and disorientation
Of a human world and maybe all the

Fuss is like a chaotic dream forcing
My adaptation and evolution —
And the balancing of my consciousness
Is a taste of cosmic play so that I

Experience the wild and outrageous
Emotions on the way to somewhere else.

Maybe I was an
Apatosaurus swinging
a mighty bullwhip tail
150 million
years ago.

This moment contains all the galaxies
And all the motions of the galaxies
And all of their suns and their planets too —
Orbits within orbits within orbits —

This is the moment of becoming when
Something new and fresh is arising
And you need not believe that what comes is
Bound by the past but you may dare to seek

A liberation perhaps not apart
From pain and disorientation or
Even terror but through difficulty
And then maybe a new freedom will come

As easily as an apple falling
From a tree — metamorphosis arrives.

Be poised
open
patient
calm
ready.

Kitcat's whiskers are unbelievable
Having supersensitive tips able
To pick up vibrations within the dark
Letting him know which objects to avoid

Whether he can fit inside of a box
Or inside of the cupboard above my
Refrigerator — and summer breezes
Coming through the screened windows of my home

Send him messages of animals in
The neighborhood and of when a rainstorm
Is approaching — and the follicles are
Deeply embedded in his skin with nerve

Endings electrically signaling his
Awareness with a touching kind of radar.

Did a Tyrannosaur
have whiskers?

These pages are like the days of a life
Bound together with a memory of
Dubious reliability with
Each page containing the brilliance of a

Summer day arising from the paper
Consisting of the texture of a tree
That in its day was tasting the sunlight
And drinking rainwater and minerals

With its roots and whatever words can do
Upon the substance of a page to bring
To life a moment of insight and joy
The expression is worthy of a life-

Time's effort in preparation for just
A moment of carefree exploration.

Beyond the
intensity and
infinity of
this moment
there is mystery.

Love and care are essential for making
A piano and a craftsman will use
Various woods like birch mahogany
Oak ebony spruce and maple and it

Takes an expert eye to choose the straight-grained
Woods without knots and patience to air dry
The wood over six months to two years and
Virtuosity of knowledge and skill

In fitting the best wood for a precise
Function as the soundboard is made of spruce
Because spruce is quite elastic and the
Maker knows in which season to harvest

The wood when it contains the least amount
Of sap and with about 10 years of growth.

Love in transition —
the studio piano
in my living room
from her grandfather
to my daughter is
waiting for space.

The playing of a taut string via the
Bridge and nut passes to the body of
The instrument where the panels of
The violin reverberate thusly

Emitting lovely waves of sound and the
Quality of music is affected
By the rigidity of connection
Between the bridge and the panels and the

Types of wood are crucial with spruce for the
Top and willow for the internal blocks
And linings and maple for the back and
Ribs and neck and the traditional "s"-

Shaped holes on the front of the body of
The violin make a resonation.

The musician
refines herself
with creative
discipline to
play joyfully.

The wet heavy snow overnight was not
As much as forecasted but was enough for
Me to rearrange a hectic schedule
To focus on the most necessary

Chores and both of my snow blowers on both
Of the driveways were able to move the
Snow as it was melting in the machines
Becoming water demonstrating that

What doesn't work on a given day may
Surprisingly produce miracles on a
Another day and I am left without
An explanation especially when

I'm often crabby when much too busy
But today I was cheerfully engaged.

Today I am grateful
to be able to use
my arms and legs
and snow blowers
to good purpose.

The voice of a harp arises from the
Plucking of the differently sized strings
Making the vibrations of higher and
Lower frequency and the playing of

The strings pushes energy onto the
Curving soundboard making vibrations of
Ascending and descending quality
And when vibrations ascend air rushes

Into the shape of the harp and when the
Vibrations descend air pushes out of
Its shape and out of the air holes along
The straight back of the instrument and the

Rippling pressures entering eardrums
With tasteful frequency make the music.

The harp is depicted
in images inside of
Egyptian and
Mesopotamian
tombs and produces
tears laughter and sleep.

The accumulation of overcast
Days with the blanketing of snow on the
Ground with the opacity of the sky
And the drab gray/brown of the leafless trees

Imposes a weariness over the
Season wherein the details of the days
Merge together in memory after
A somewhat happy day of moving snow

Off of driveways I know that yesterday
Will dissolve as surely as one falling
Of snow will blend with the snow on the ground
Without a seam as the streets become a

Patchwork of cleared asphalt and ice and the
Chickadees and the crows are spicing days.

After 24 years of
moving snow the
corners of my
iron shovel are
rusted and curled.

When I'm meditating he sleeps on the
Couch in the living room with me and he
Will sometimes while I'm meditating sprawl
And stretch out on the rug in front of me

Just to distract my attention and on
Saturday and on Sunday the only
Days when I don't set the alarm at 5
A.m. he will yowl and cavort on the

Bed much earlier than I intend to
Get up and if I don't get out of bed
Then he will jump on the chest of drawers and
Lick and nibble on the peacock feathers

That I keep in a marble urn because
He knows exactly how to annoy me.

Brushing Kitcat
after I leave bed is the
pinnacle of the
day when he wrestles
yowls and bites.

I was enlightened while digging up the
Information necessary to write
Poetry about dinosaurs when I read
That both cats and Tyrannosaurus Rex

Have an ample percentage of their brains
Devoted to a sense of smell and with
A new awareness I've been watching how
Kitcat will sniff just about everything

Over again including my hands and
Maybe my hands do smell differently
At various times which naturally
Leads me to imagine a curious

And rather insistent Tyrannosaur
Sniffing my hands which isn't very nice.

My living room
is much too small
to contain a T-Rex.

There is the belief that whatever we
Obsess over we draw into our lives
And I think I am safe concerning an
Obsequious Tyrannosaurus Rex

And I also believe haphazardly
Without quite intending it I've gotten
Better at attracting beneficial
Instead of detrimental involvements

Into my experience because I
Spend so much of my time cogitating
Mostly curious and optimistic
Poetry as I am hunting for those

Special moments happening everyday
That are worthy of a celebration.

The little red squirrel
that I watch run along
the top of the white fence
down the hill *came* to the hedge
just outside of my window.

Even during the somnolent season
When the ground is blanketed with the snow
And the sky is so often overcast
Outside my window where I am typing

On my keyboard and composing my thoughts
The days are peppered with inspiration
As the hedge trimmed below the windowsill
Is little more than a foot from me and

Within these couple of hours today
The little red squirrel and a female
Cardinal and three differently marked
Chickadees came to peek at me moving

As they do in jerky hopping motions
And they linger only a few seconds.

It's easy to spot
simple marvels
within
eyesight.

What would it be like to be a writer
For the Hollywood entertainment crowd
Dreaming up the scenarios and the
Dialogue for daily situation

Comedies or the soap operas or
The late-night talk shows as it would become
A daunting challenge to come up with fresh
Material garnered from everyday

Events of a quality to enthrall
The type of audience patronizing
Such shows as a writer would be impelled
To shoehorn his consciousness inside of

The ridiculous and the exploitive
The snarky corrosive and prurient?

Is making people laugh
serious
exhausting
dispiriting
drudgery?

I would like to believe myself to be
Above the prurient and corrosive
Influences of the entertainment
Industry but I am as attracted

To sarcasm as anyone is and
I admit that watching T.V. is like
Ingesting too much sugar inspiring
A temporary thrill but leading to

A depressing eventuality
So I usually confine myself
To murder investigations starting
With a gruesome mystery proceeding

With a determined pursuit of the clues
And concluding with righteous judgment.

My head is cluttered
with stories inside
stories inside
stories.

We are connected to our culture with
The Internet and are saturated
With narratives of acceptable and
Disfavored opinions and people have

Been led to distrust the "conspiracy
Theories" but each of us inherits a
Core set of beliefs honestly and we
Add to our understanding as best we

Can but these days the invective and the
Raw hatred expressed by the combatting
Parties is at an extreme and it seems
Impossible to escape bitterness

Disorientation and suspicion
As it's difficult to know whom to trust.

It's easier among
my friends who have
various opinions
not to talk about
certain topics.

I am connected to the Internet
Gathering information and doing
Business and driving about every day
With a smartphone inside of my pocket

And Google Facebook and Amazon are
Collecting information and tracking
My whereabouts and are following my
Use of the Internet as one of three

Hundred million Americans and
I do assume that with such a massive
Number of people that I have privacy
And protective anonymity with

Nothing to fear no reason for worry
As who would care about how I'm living?

Our sophisticated
information
society is
increasingly
interconnected.

If I am not carefully watching the
Power of my thinking I will become
A mighty iron freight engine pulling
A weighty train of cars and each car will

Encapsulate a memory of a
Vanished opportunity or of an
Argument involving bitter words or
A rehearsal of justifications

And my mighty engine will run along
The iron rails of negativity
Oblivious to the liberation
That comes with simple relaxation as

For some reason it is easy to be
Angry but so difficult to relax.

When I am lost
in a memory I'm
not using my
eyes to see or
my ears to hear.

There are always details to attend to
And chores of necessity to finish
And snares of difficulty and if I
Worry I can be like Alice falling

Down an endless rabbit hole and dreading
A hard landing but this morning snow is
Curving to the ground in tiny grains and
The flakes are meandering and lazy

And there isn't any wind and the air
Is much colder today as it should be
In January which means that the snow
Will be light and easy to move and now

I am watching the snow mix with the sky
And the meandering snow is the sky.

The snow/sky
or sky/snow
is glowing
white with
sunlight.

I have to take off the elephantine
Mittens to press the tiny button of
The car keys to open the door of the
Car and then I buckle the seatbelt with

My hands and insert the key into the
Ignition and start the car and I put
On the mittens again because of
The cold but soon I get to the office

And take off the mittens to press on the
Button of the garage door opener
And I exit the car opening doors
With one hand holding stapled papers and

The two thermoses of coffee and the
Two mittens with the other handy hand.

I press the thermoses
and stapled papers
to my body under
the crook of a
bent elbow.

My kids are grown and are making their way
In the world and they have my affection —
My ex-wife and I are living apart
After having raised our kids together

And she and I are better off apart —
And the weight of the care of having a
Family earning a precarious
Income making repairs as best I could

Schooling the kids celebrating birthdays
Taking vacations lying awake in
Bed with worry about their struggles and
Their health — all these apprehensions have passed —

My solitary putzing about the
House is assuming a Zen quietude.

I talk with friends
see birds
apple blossoms
autumn leaves
shadows on snow.

Driving along the street to the office
Which I do absentmindedly daily
I am seeing this morning the line of
Oaks and cottonwoods bordering the street

As the sun is cresting the horizon
To the right and I don't see rays of
Light in the air but I do see the bare
Trees bathed in a glow of orange sunlight

And I am the only one present as
The street is empty of traffic and hushed
And for some reason I am impacted
By the light with joyful solemnity

As if all my burdens were lifted for
A moment by a touch of loveliness.

Glimpsing beauty
amid a drab
landscape — joy
takes me.

Clouds

Stratus — low layering horizontal
Cirrus — wispy curling locks of hair
Stratocumulus — large dark rounded and low
Cumulonimbus — towering vertical thunderheads
Cumulus — cottonlike
Altostratus — gray to bluish-green layers
Nimbostratus — continuous rain snow sleet
Altocumulus — globs masses patches
Cirrocumulus — high patches and rows
Cirrostratus — high thin diffuse

We name the
continuous drama
of earth sun
oceans rivers
atmosphere.

The saying goes that the Great Way isn't
Difficult for those without preferences
As it is a disease of the mind to
Cherish opinions arguing against

Offensive ideas with opposing
Ideas endlessly and even the
Burning intensity of love propels
Its opposite hate which corrodes the heart

Dispirits equanimity and I
Understand the wording of the "Heart/Mind"
Sutra asserting that once the mind is
Emptied everything else vanishes but

I can't see how meditation empties
The mind or if I want to be empty.

I enjoy
coffee
with cream.

It is easy to believe that I am
Somebody going somewhere doing my
Best to make someone of myself and with
Extra effort I can accomplish a

Goal and afterward I will relax and
Be proud of myself as I can vaguely
Remember a beginning and I am
Certain there's an ending and now I seem

To be somewhere in the middle but for
Some reason the poetry breaks
The rules as there isn't a narrative
Binding poems together but rather

Every poem is curiosity
Tasting and savoring differing vibes.

Maybe I am
a conscious
ripple within
ripples within
ripples.

The crows aren't bothered by the arctic cold
As they don't feel the need to move about
As they are busy perching in the oak
As light is rising from the horizon

Behind them and they get my attention
By vibrating air with their voices and
I notice the rippling resonance in
The air and I see them perching on what

Seem to me the thinnest of the twigs of
The bur oak and I realize that the
Crows know better than I how much weight a
Twig will bear and suddenly one of the

Crows leaves the oak and flies to a maple
Perhaps to sound his voice from over there.

The two crows
in the park
at sunrise
are a joy
this morning.

It's been pointed out to me that I am
Not as affectionate as I could be
As I appear emotionally distant and
Reserved in person and I know it's true

And I feel an awkward self-consciousness
About touching and embracing others
And even though I'm able to smile in
Carefree conversation it's difficult

To relax and put on a natural
Expression for a photograph so I
Sport at best a grin or look impassive
Because somehow I've become defensive

And I'm wearing a suit of armor as
A tool against vulnerability.

Unlearning
unconscious
unintentional
habits is
tricky.

The words are skipping across the paper
In a horizontal fashion from the
Left and to the right and the words are a
Trick manipulating you my reader

To follow the flow of the words to form
The syllables silently perhaps and
To register ideas as you are
Shifting your eyes from left to right reaching

The end of a line and dropping to the
Line below following a train of thought
Anticipating by now where is this
Package of verbiage leading and what

Is its purpose and what does it really mean
And I will say it's just a dance of words . . .

. . . as the seconds
and the minutes and
the hours are just a
dance of days.

An overcast winter sky resembles
The whiteness of a page with an added
Tinge of gray and the bareness of the trees
Is similar to letters on a page

Because the dark branches and black letters
Appear upon a white background and the
Contrast is rather stark but the letters
Are symmetrical and regimented

And the words are logical and carry
Meaning — at least the meaning is implied —
Whereas the forms of the trees under a
Winter sky have no symmetry at all

And maybe their twisting and crooked forms
Epitomize wild creativity.

The nonsymmetrical
wild creativity
evolved into logic
but what does that
mean?

According to scientists maybe the
Most telling act of creativity
Within the more than four billion years of
The spinning Earth was accomplished by a

Prokaryote which is a single-celled
Organism possessing a membrane
But not a nucleus which was the first
Living organism that somehow learned

To use its body to catch photons from
The sun creating photosynthesis
Starting the ball rolling without a brain
Or eyes or hands or blueprints and without

Any foresight or consciousness and thus
All of our complexities have blossomed.

All the questions
scientists can
dream of
originated from
a senseless blob.

So did the chickadee pecking about
In the hedge outside of my window come
Into the world from somewhere else or did
The chickadee come out of the world

And did I projecting as I do a
Frolicsome curiosity and a
Burdensome load of anxiety come
Into the world from somewhere else or did

I come out of the world as a consequence
Of a cosmic eruption emerging
From incomprehensible nothingness
Proceeding with orbits within orbits

Ripples within ripples within ripples
And destined to return to nothingness?

Is nothingness itself
somewhere else
or is it here?

After a powder snow the white of snow
And the white sky and the white of the page
Overwhelm the neighborhood coating the
Needles of the pines and the branches of

The trees and concealing the grime and grit
Filling bootprints and squirrel tracks and I
Yank the cord start the blower raise its front
Pull back and turn directing it squeezing

Its handles engaging its rotor blades
And I am methodically plowing
The snow in straight lines just like the words of
This poem as the words are progressing

From the left to the right I am pacing
Happily clearing the driveway of snow.

Snow covers everything
I plow the snow
in straight lines
and type words
in straight lines.

A fresh falling of snow erases the
Accumulating mess that snow becomes
Over winter days and the crud that drops
From the wheel wells of cars is hidden and

The pitting and misshaping that thawing
And freezing does to snow on the ground is
Covered and when the sky clears again then
Suddenly the trees are casting patterns

Of wild shadows across the pristine snow
And sunlight descending from an open
Sky is sparking embedded crystals of snow
Making pinpoint gleams of green blue and red

And then the snow is appearing to be
An enchanting mesmerizing blanket.

But even inside a
house I have to wear
thick winter socks
to warm
my toes.

"Woo" is a wonderful word for the art
Of persuasion in love when a lover
Is possessed by a passion enraptured
Dazzled besotted with a beloved

And wooing is a multiplication
Of adoration during the day and
Of enticing exciting entwining
Dreams in the night and to woo is be

Captured by "foo" and when one is moved to
Wooing it's all based upon a fooing
Without a smidgeon of moderation
And when I am wooing it is because

I can't escape from the fooing and all
Of my awareness is consumed with foo.

I don't believe
it's possible to
woo unless one
is saturated with
foo.

Someone should not spend too much of his time
Doing business under the influence
Of foo because foo is nonsensical
And foo is befuddlement and when one

Is apart from his rationality
One is liable to foozle over
A crazy choice of words and to foozle
In using his money and one might say

That fooing and wooing lead directly
To foozlement because when one is in
Love sobriety is an afterthought
And it's not unheard of for someone to

Be foozling haphazardly and I
Can attest to my own share of foozle.

Can you imagine
a woozy
foozy
doctor
judge
scientist
politician?

I am not a propitious judge of
The worthiness of my conversation
Of the clarity of my editing
Or of the value of my poetry

Because on occasion I assume that
My facility of expression is
Jubilant and the words are of themselves
Falling logically into proper

Order but upon a second reading
A glaring error will batter me about
My brain and I will feel as low as dirt
And I may be downhearted for many

Days doubting every syllable I choose
Questioning my sincerity of voice.

Riding waves and troughs
whether up or down
I'm attempting
to be
diligent.

I have a quirky dictionary with
Eccentric curious exotic words
And when lacking fresh ideas I may
Utter "jobbernowl" instead of blockhead

Or "ratbaggery" when meaning nonsense
Or "cantabank" in description of a
Mediocre balladeer — or poet —
But I would rather not have to depend

On splendiferous words to make a point
As it's better to say ordinary
Words in good order with an intention
Of expressing something worth the effort

Of reading which means I have to study
Phenomena carefully faithfully.

Queequeg the harpooner
seen through the eyes
of Ishmael in
Moby Dick is
fascinating.

There was no explanation for me to
Be so downhearted when I was so young
And had just graduated from college
Without debt after having spent my last

Year in Oxford England imbibing the
Best of the literature the English
Could offer there was no sane rationale
For the despondency I fell into

Other than my being alcoholic
Which meant that I drank to alleviate
Oppressive thinking which only served to
Give my oppressive thoughts a better grip

But I turned my life around by hitting
Bottom and by practicing principles.

A ride with the police
a detox center
a treatment center
a halfway house
a sober house
started a journey.

I can't reliably remember
The details of my thinking 40 years
Ago other than saying I was in
A treatment center for a month and a

Halfway house for five months and then I got
A room in a sober house and didn't
Have a job but was sober and meeting
With other sober drunks and I made a

A new beginning but without the numbing
Effect of alcohol I discovered
Fear fed resentment fed self-pity fed
Fear fed resentment fed self-pity fed

A barrage of oppressive emotions
And I didn't have an answer for it.

With my whole life ahead
young intelligent and free
I dug myself a
pit of misery
to hide in.

The other guys in the sober house were
Doing their best as I was but people
Who live in sober houses are starting
On perilous journeys and they are not

Entirely sane and we each took turns
Cleaning a cat litterbox but someone
Refused to do the job and I wouldn't
Because it wasn't my turn so the house

Began to fester and I didn't care
Because I was busy sleeping all day
And all night and the only reason I
Got out of bed was to have breakfast which

I did by going to a McDonald's
Restaurant that was luckily next door.

I remember
paper cups of coffee
with cream —
pancakes
with maple syrup
on Styrofoam plates.

I salvaged myself unexpectedly
By reading Herman Melville's *Moby Dick*
And in the beginning Ishmael says
When he gets a little grim about the

Mouth upon the land it's time for him to
Return to the sea and board a whaling
Vessel and on an icy blizzarding
Night Ishmael went to the Spouter Inn

With almost empty pockets and was forced
To share a bed with a tattooed savage
Queequeg a harpooner who was selling
Severed heads in New Bedford and who slept

With a tomahawk which also served him
As a tobacco pipe at his leisure.

I drank my self-obsession
away with many paper
cups of coffee with cream
by reading *Moby Dick*
at McDonald's.

Resolving to fix the litter box I
Tied a bandana about my face to
Suppress my sense of smell which was useless
And ineffective but I got busy

Becoming a waiter and a cashier
And doing other odd jobs while riding
The number 16 bus between St. Paul
And Minneapolis where I found the

Jewish Vocational Center along
University Avenue which led
To a book *Jobs in Japan* that explained
The process of getting a job teaching

English in the private language schools that
Were eagerly recruiting fresh teachers.

I boarded an airplane
and landed in Osaka
learning katakana
on the flight — not knowing
anyone in Japan.

I favor granola with blueberries
And slices of banana for breakfast
And it's a marvel of modern days that
We may find at Aldi's the cheapest of

Grocery stores blueberries coming from
Chile in January during a
Global pandemic and bananas are
OK though maybe not as exotic

And they spoil precipitously from bright
Yellow ripeness to deplorable brown
Spots on the peel and on the fruit so I
Scrounge for the bunches of green bananas

Of six or seven enough to last a
Week before they become inedible

I like a proper
amount of banana
but not too much
so I choose
small green bananas.

I believe with all my heart in nothing
And observation and evidence are
Accumulating of the cruelty
The arguing and indifference of

People between people along with willful
Ignorance including my own fickle
Eccentricities so it is hard to
Put much faith in human institutions

And I was nothing before being born
And I will become nothing after death
But somehow I am the most marvelous
Something now defying explanation

And there isn't a creation myth that
Encompasses the fact of no-thing-ness.

I am optimistic
because something
is always coming
from nothing.

Don't expect my poetry to involve
A continuing narrative from page
To page as each poem embodies its
Own cosmos and I am not attempting

To contrive a cohesive perspective
Throughout a series of pages and if
You are sensing a consistent point of
View that is because the whirlpool of a

Personality is quite similar
From day to day but my intention is
To describe a world where each happening
Is interwoven with every other

Happening without separation and
So much happens simultaneously.

The seeds of tomorrow's
growth are already
in the ground as
much is passing
away.

I appreciate the dexterity
Of my fingers because I was born with
Them and didn't do anything to earn
Their use and almost everything I do

Involves their precise sensitivity
And they create such delicacy and
So much — if not all — of my sense of touch
Is felt with the tips of my fingers and

I cannot imagine tying my shoes
Or buttoning my shirt or cutting an
Apple or feeling the texture of fleece
Or scratching my nose or typing on a

Keyboard with my toes as my toes don't do
Anything besides filling out my shoes.

I also touch
the horizon the birds
the clouds and with a
glimpse the sunrise
with my eyes.

When I am slicing a banana for
My breakfast I am happiest when not
Thinking about anything other than
Slicing a banana for my breakfast

And in fact when I am only slicing
A banana and not thinking about
Any other random obsession that
Catches me at odd moments then it is

True that I am not thinking at all but
Am only slicing a banana for
Breakfast and it is good to be doing
Something useful with my body without

The complexity of having to think
About it — which just might make me grumpy.

Do you think a
Tyrannosaur
taking a bite of
a Triceratops
was thinking about it?

Segmentation is a bane of my
Existence as I direct energy
According to the hours of a day
Consistent with the days within a month

As I need to accomplish business with
The benefit of morning clarity
Which turns the challenge of complexity
Into child's play and to manage the broad

Sweep of activity I have to watch
The dates of my publishing schedule and
Have to attend to the 15th of the
Month when I pay myself and my bills

As being a human seems to involve
The regimentation of enterprise.

The leafing of a tree
the growth of a tomato
the hunger of a
Tyrannosaur don't
involve human time.

I have seen the movies inspired by
The lure of "Jurassic Park" where the mad
And the irresponsible scientists
Brought the dinosaurs back to life using

Scraps of DNA with the intention
Of making money from tourists of the
Park and I can't get the image of the
Bald-pated Tyrannosaur out of mind

As he appears vaguely similar to
The sinewy and acrobatic bald-
Headed *karate* thugs so commonplace
In the movies but do you suppose that

A Tyrannosaur was really bald or
Might he not have had fur or feathers?

The uselessness of
a Tyrannosaur's
puny little arms
is puzzling and
funny.

My fingers and toes are so delicate
And easily harmed by inattentive
Clumsiness around the iron dumbbell
That I've positioned within my living

Room and who's to blame when I swing and smash
My toes against the unbudgeable mass
Of metal plopped on the floor under the
Edge of the coffee table or when I

Reach for the dumbbell without attending
Carefully to the speed and direction
Of my hand — and then I wince and bear a
Surge of painful toes or pinky finger

Reminding me that my appendages
Will sharply penalize my carelessness.

Did T. Rex
ever pinch
or jam a
puny arm?

I wonder whether we could attribute
The elements of personality
To a Tyrannosaur because I see
Evidence of character in Kitcat

As Kitcat will paw and disturb letters
That I keep in a bowl on my table
With the goal of seizing my attention
And Kitcat will leap onto the top of

My refrigerator and caterwaul
At me exerting I believe in his
Mind a dominance over me and I
Have read that both tyrannosaurs and cats

Possess an enhanced sense of smell so could
A Tyrannosaur have been quirky too?

How could a
Tyrannosaur be
quirky without
first thinking of
eating everyone?

Bald-pated Tyrannosaur you can't catch me
You may lumber and roar and crush a car
You may snarl with your teeth like scimitars
You stomp and blunder but can't bite me
You may shake your head but you can't get me
You may very well be the king of beasts
With every creature comprising a feast
You rule the forest but can't swallow me
With all your majesty you can't touch me
You may trot and gambol and have a ball
You stomp and smash and rip and tear and maul
But whatever you do you can't catch me
And wherever you go you won't see me
Because you are now extinct don't you see?

P.S. A Tyrannosaur may
crush cars in future movies.

Tyrannosaurs in Requiem

He gamboled upon the earth
He expressed plenty of mirth
But he's had his day
And it's fair to say
He won't have another birth.

I would not be the person who I am
Without reading the sonnets of Shakespeare
Even though I've come to see the crazy
Houdini-encumbering rhyming scheme

At the ends of his lines to be a waste
Of effort and a frustration of free
Expression but nevertheless the pith
And passion of his lovely delicate

Little poems indelibly affected
Me — and I wouldn't be who I am if
I hadn't read Japanese poetry

As they astonished me by putting so
Much sensitivity in so few words.

Shakespeare and
the Japanese
fashion poetry
like keenly
sharp daggers.

I also would not be exploring the
World as I do today if I hadn't
Absorbed *Siddhartha* by the novelist
Hermann Hesse as the suffering and the

Questing to end suffering with the use
Of meditation reverberated
As I was perusing pages in a
High school library — and I might have been

Swallowed up in a mire of self-pity
If I hadn't had the exquisite shock
Of reading Herman Melville's *Moby Dick*
That made me forget myself entirely

By enticing me with the exotic
Narrative of Ishmael the sailor.

Two Hermans
moved me
by writing
vibrantly.

To get a laugh from my friends in every
Month of last year I have touted my post-
Traumatic February Disorder
And today is February 1st and

Not a phantom put-on February
But a real February so I pulled
On the long underwear to go under
My jeans and slipped on two pairs of socks and

Two hats and elephantine mittens and
Drove to the park for my outdoor meeting
And saw a touch of ice on the concrete
From yesterday's drizzle but it was just

A little below freezing as I was
Wrapped like an eggroll and feeling silly.

Reality is
usually
different
from what
I think.

We gathered around the cheery fire in
Our container at Pioneer Park and
Began our meeting of sober drunks with
The view of Stillwater below us and

Of the winding river valley into
The distance and coincident with our
Conversation one of us heard the spring
Songs of an American Crow of a

Black-capped chickadee of a white-breasted
Nuthatch and of a Northern Cardinal
But I only recognized the crow as
My ears are not very sensitive and

As we were each speaking — one at a
Time — I did hear the Northern Cardinal.

Without Fran
alerting us to the
cardinal I would
never have
heard it.

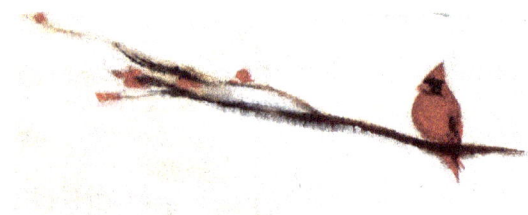

At our Monday morning meeting we talk
About yesterday and tomorrow and
Today with the point being that to live
Well in today we need freedom from the

Burdens of yesterday and tomorrow
From remorse and anxiety which are
Phantoms of the mind as for some reason
It is easy to be negative and

Hard to be optimistic just as it's
Easy to hear a crow but tricky to
Pick up the cardinal as I needed
Direction to hear the cardinal and

So I need to practice principles and
Rely on a power greater than me.

We have already
made it through most
of our first year of
hobo meetings
in the park.

At the beginning of February
Under an overcast sky within a
Culture that is intoxicated with
Technology and media and the

News cycle it's easy to forget that
The earth the sun and the moon are doing
Their interweaving dance beyond the clouds
And tomorrow in the north we will reach

The midmost point between the winter and
Spring equinoxes which the Celtic tribes
Celebrated with a festival as
"Imbolc" or "Brigid's day" for the marking

Of the beginning of spring even as
The ground is quiescent under the snow.

The weaving
of fire air
water earth
continues
quietly.

Perhaps the roots of the trees are waking
And seeds in the ground are poised for growing
And the bears in their dens are stirring as
Daylight is arising earlier and

Lasting longer into the evening but
The cold is persistent and heavy on
The land impelling yet a sheltering
Indoors and a separation from the

Zest of activity sweating under
A blazing sun and thusly this is a
Time for asking what is essential and
What is no longer worthy of doing

And how are circumstances transforming
And how do I need to adapt myself?

The opacity
of an overcast
sky is weighty
with questions.

Am I working hard to accomplish goals?
Has enough of my stridency been tamed?
Do I still need to prove my worth to me?
And I have only to ask the questions

To understand the effort involved in
Making something of myself by getting
Ahead of the competition using
The vigor of focused intelligence

To be proud and comfortable later
And I really don't know how to behave
Differently as society does
Impose its pressures but a part of me

Is exhausted and dissatisfied and
Blundering about for liberation.

Random thought
mesmerizing
emotion
keeps
happening.

It's 2 a.m. and the cat wants to play
As he is gamboling upon my bed
Pouncing and biting until I say "hey
It's way too early and you have been fed"
As I'm feeling the pulsation of blood
Throbbing at my temples on the pillow
And Kitcat jumps to the floor with a thud
And what he thinks he's doing yes I know
Because I've gotten him used to playing
When I will rise from bed before the dawn
When I brush and rub him while I'm singing
When he loves his brushing and has his fun
When he gets excited and wants to fight
When I slap his paws and he tries to bite.

Kitcat had reason
to think I was getting up
from sleeping because
I rose from bed twice
to write notes for a poem.

I dread the twilight zone in the middle
Of the night when I wake from sleeping and
My mind has the opportunity to
Run away with me and this morning I

Was drowsy on the edge of slumber yet
Nervous energy from yesterday was
Enough to spur a subconscious hunt for
Exorbitant words for a trivial

Poem and in my ambivalence thoughts
Acquired metal-studded cleats that poked
Into my consciousness and compelled my
Rising from bed to scrawl syllables on

Notepaper because I can't rely on
Nighttime memory to survive the night.

A tinge of agony
over whether I should
rise and make a note
or forget the thought
tends to wake me up.

When I pinch the tires of my bicycle
Laid against the chairs in my dining room
I detect squishiness instead of the
Roadworthy firmness that I desire and

Seeing the bicycle laid staidly in
My dining room everyday has had a
Subconscious and subversive influence
On my temperament as winter drags on

As the stationary bike within my
Living room has provided a sturdy
Service as I have listened to music
On headphones and pumped my legs for an hour

Every day but I want to face the wind
Again and climb the hill into Houlton.

I am looking forward
to hearing peeper frogs
and seeing tulips
from my bike
in the spring.

The branches of the
maple are swaying in
the wind under a
shining blue sky but
snow comes tomorrow.

—*Tekkan*

Everyday Mind XIX

Morning light
spreads
bitter cold
penetrates.

Words
are
incapable
of describing
the wild
gesturing
of
leafless
winter
trees.

The indigo bunting migrates at night
Following stars for orientation
Adjusting the angle guiding its flight
Taking its bearings from constellations
The brilliant bluest blue of all the birds
Its feathers refract and reflect the light
Its beauty far surpasses all my words
Seeing it suddenly is a delight
The birds will return sometime within May
To flit and frolic on the edge of woods
But its image is helping me today
To overcome my frigid winter moods
The birds nest in roadside thickets fields streams
They also resonate in winter dreams.

February snow
minutely sparkles with
the brightest sunlight
but eventually I
get tired of seeing the snow.

I think today is Super Bowl Sunday
And by quickly perusing with Google
I learn the Kansas City Chiefs will play
The Tampa Bay Buccaneers for boodle
Forty years ago I did like football
My team was the Minnesota Vikings
The Purple People Eaters stood so tall
They destroyed the offense with me cheering
The Vikings went to the Super Bowl twice
And I was enamored and excited
But twice they were humbled like little mice
And I was depressed and disappointed
I think sometimes if the Vikings had won
My entire life would have been more fun.

The Vikings lost not
twice but four times at the
Super Bowl and I
was crushed and haven't watched an
hour of football ever since.

Over my everyday underwear I
Put on both the tops and the bottoms of
My long underwear and I slip on a
Pair of warm socks but they are not enough

Then I don my thickest pair of jeans and
A winter fleece that protects my torso
And arms and wraps quite snuggly about my
Neck and I even wrap a scarf around

My neck and then I slip on the knitted
Socks and insert my feet in the bulky
Winter boots and get inside of my down
Jacket and put on a knitted hat that

Covers my ears and put on a Knitted
Hood grab my mittens and go out the door.

Our meeting at Pioneer
Park for an hour on
Monday morning for
conversation is a
crazy extravagance.

It is 93 million miles away
And I know because of modern science
It was orange when at the horizon
But now it is a blazing burning white

The sky is a cloudless and a pale blue
The snow on the ground is starting to shine
Millions of embedded crystals are lit
The more I look the more gleams I'm seeing

I'm 63 years old but now I am
Young because I am not worried about
Anything and the branches of the trees
Are motionless and the land is quiet

All the branches of the trees are crooked
Appearing natural and beautiful.

Even at my desk
at my window
even with thick socks
the bitter cold
is freezing my toes.

The alarm is triggered at 5 a.m.
And the jingle is quite inoffensive
In fact if I were to choose a tune to
Fall asleep with this would be the warble

And to turn the alarm off I have to
Press upon four squares in numerical
Order on my tablet and to do that
I have to commit to waking up to

Experience the wrenching transition
From a dream of wild adventure or of
Adoration where I was the center
Of heavenly attention back to dull

Reality wherein I have to choose
Whether to get up or return to sleep.

I start my days
groggy
doleful and
disgruntled.

The overhang between sleep and daytime
Awareness is often not such a stark
Transition for me when I find myself
Awake an hour or several hours

Before the dawn when I discover that
Thoughts will run away with my consciousness
When I would much rather be asleep but
Instead I am dwelling on arguments

Or broken relationships or vanished
Opportunities and I have chosen
Sometimes to be a captive of my thoughts
And sometimes I will turn to spiritual

Jujitsu when I rise and assume the
Lotus posture for some meditation.

A simple posture
of the body
positions me
to dissipate
unwanted thoughts.

I would very much like to meet the guy
Who is acting as me inside of my
Dreams as he is the sort of person who
Stands calmly upon the dizzy top of

An alpine mountain in a wingsuit and
Jumps enabling me to imagine
Flying in and out of gargantuan
Alpine shadows and I am having fun

Teasing and taunting Kitcat every day
But he cracks a bullwhip and challenges
Lions and tigers inside of a cage
And the most dangerous activity

I do is driving on the highway but
Volcanoes are in his vicinity.

I would trade
my tranquility
for his
vulnerability
in a heartbeat.

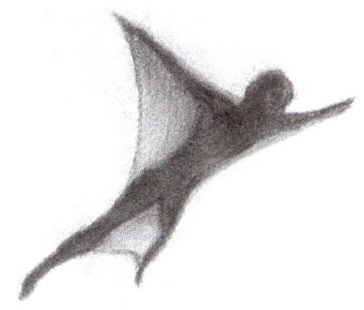

The adventurous fellow in my dreams
Is my avatar weaving symbolic
Subconscious and nightly commentary
Perhaps as dramatic counterpoise to

My ordinary existence and his
Emotions are intense as he loves more
Vividly and gets more terrified than
I do but I suspect my wakeful self

Is much more meditative as I'm not
A whirl of activity and it is
Not so easy to identify which
Of my emotions I am feeling

As I feel emotions differently
As anger resonates along my spine.

I sleep with my
left ear on the pillow
and my left ear
gets plugged
with wax.

The same trees are gesturing outside of
My window every day and if I'm not
Careful if I am busy with the news
Entangling myself with loathing and with

Disgust then the obvious winter trees
Immersed within their dormancy become
Invisible and meaningless to me
But I may return to my body and

Attend to breathing lungs and a beating
Heart and gaze at the unsymmetrical
Brilliance of the crooked and the twisting
Quality of winter trees beyond my

Comprehension as there isn't any
Pattern or design to grasp ahold of.

The leafless trees
exhibit a wild
explosion of
creative
genius.

Imagine if time were variable
And thus you could see within a minute
A tree sprouting and spurting upward from
The ground observing the wiggling and the

Sudden shocking sideways outthrusting of
Its limbs splaying out in its dozens of
Unpredictable directions in an
Explosion of growth and then the finest

And minutest details of the twigs would
Emerge like capillaries all for the
Aiming of individual leaves for
The tasting and absorption of sunlight

As the trees appearing in winter are
A testament to creativity.

Something about
sunlight and soil
prompts the crooked
twisting of
trees.

But such an instantaneous insight
Of an explosive growth of a tree would
Be an injustice to the solicitous
And tenuous exploration of air

On the part of the tree as one wonders
What does the sunlight do to earth and soil
To engender such creativity
As the open sky is revealed to be

A progenitor with the sun and the
Universe and the thing that went bang that
Impelled the cosmos eventually
To arrive at a point where a person

Contemplates just so much interweaving
Of a crazy phantasmagoria.

I am saturated
with the
identical
impetus of
creativity.

I'm back in Pioneer Park on Friday
Temperature minus thirteen degrees
Fahrenheit wrapped inside of layers of
Clothing like an eggroll exuberant

With the extravagance of biweekly
Camaraderie and conversation
With only my cheeks and nose exposed to
The cold as we talk about the joys of

Living without alcohol as the sun
Is cresting the horizon and we are
Discussing who we have harmed and how we
Intend to make amends for the damage

Because that is what we desire to do
To free ourselves from the burden of guilt.

The wide river valley
stretches southward
and a crow's caw
reverberates.

When I have the luxury of being
Free of the compulsion of having to
Do some necessary chore so that it
Is possible to lounge and look out of

The window and watch the drama of the
Clouds and the flights of birds each peculiar
To their species then I often note the
Quiet presence of the trees and I love

To mix their unsymmetrical beauty
With the sensation of my beating heart
The throbbing of blood in my veins and the
Rhythmic pattern of my breathing with the

Awareness that the vibrations of my
Body are interwoven with the earth.

Accumulating snow
fresh snow
bitter cold
make for
a meditative
trance.

The sky isn't completely covered with
Clouds as wind-shredded openings appear
But the clouds are dominating the sky
At the moment and I find it pleasant

To remind myself that even when the
Sun isn't visible the clouds glow white
Because of the eminence of the sun
And I can close my eyes while facing the

Window on a bitter cold day and my
Eyelids are red and also infused with
Penetrating sunlight and I also
Sense the pulsation of my eyes and of

My whole body as if the sun itself
Were the vibrating and pulsating source.

The burning of the sun
and the pulsation
of my body are
simpatico.

The concatenation of the human world
Crazed bickering insatiable
Is on parade in the news media
And it's helpful to take a holiday

From the disturbing issues as long as
Someone doesn't come along to take
A bite out of me or of someone whom
I love wherein there is my dilemma

That I do need to follow the drift of
Society but it's beneficial
To lounge and return to the beating of
My heart and the breathing of my lungs and

The wind has swept the clouds from the sky
And the shadows of trees lie on fresh snow.

Fresh gleaming snow
A million pinpoint jewels
of red green blue
are permutations of
a burning sun.

I am pondering whether the beating
Of my heart and the pulsation of my
Body are more than simpatico with
The eminence of the sun and whether

The sun itself is burning vibrating
And pulsating perhaps not in rhythmic
Harmony with human or animal
Hearts but on a different frequency

With the sun imposing its dominance
Rippling warming heating scorching with the
Winter trees responding gradually
In a rhythm of dormancy and of

Leafy vibrancy and whether the whole
Earth is a dance of waving particles.

When I close my eyelids
and sense pulsation
am I only sensing
my body and not
the sun?

Humans manipulate the vibration
Of sounds with violins cellos harps and
Mighty church organs and I can almost
Imagine seeing the vibrant rippling of

Sound impacting in the air as the earth
Exhibits its own tuneful resonance
For instance the return of breezes in
Springtime leaves with voices both profoundly

Joyful or mournful depending upon
My mood and there are innumerable
Continuing reverberations as
For example earlier this morning

The sky was overcome with smothering
Clouds but blusters have swept the clouds away.

Igneous
metamorphic
sedimentary rocks
are a rhythm
of earthly becoming.

The Northern Cardinal doesn't migrate
It fluffs its feathers and endures the cold
In February its calls will vibrate
As the mating of the male becomes bold
Fluttering swooping gliding it appears
A scarlet flash amid the pristine snow
A loveliness of red and white cohere
In an instant a marvelous tableau
A cardinal in winter is a gift
In the middle of a frigid season
Hungry and scavenging it must persist
It is beautiful without a reason
It's exceedingly odd the way things are
That such beauty exists is quite bizarre.

Latent energy
lies dormant inside of the
gnarly contorted
branches of a winter tree
as a cardinal perches.

My head is exhausted so I'm quitting
Scrounging for words is a dreary business
Working so hard while stoically sitting
Fussing with syllables is an illness
Attempting to rhyme contorts the grammar
Very often the meaning makes no sense
Pounding out rhymes with a ball peen hammer
Waiting for ideas creates suspense
I've had too much coffee now I'm weary
My acuity is out the window
I really do want to take it easy
All I can do now is mumbo-jumbo
I am very tired and it's time to quit
Don't especially care if words don't fit.

It is such a waste of time
Straining and trying to rhyme
They're kind of a crutch
They don't mean much
And the poems aren't worth a dime.

Lily the calico cat comes downstairs
To greet me with a grumpy yowling that
Is her way of saying hello after
I get to my desk and window in the

Morning and perhaps her intention is
No more than to expostulate "look at
Me here I am again" — so I yowl with
A rising questioning inflection or

I remark "what do you want?" in people
Language and if she's close enough I will
Grab her and put her on the desk where she
Takes dainty steps upon the scattered sheets

Of paper while jabbering or she may
Sit looking out the window like I do.

Some of us are
irascible within
contented
satisfaction.

With flutters the Black-capped chickadees come
To the feeder in the cold with sideways
Glimpses at each other pecking at the
Seed watching puffing feathers snatching the

Wire mesh with their feet with one asserting
Dominance with one forced to fly away
As the two remaining chickadees hop
Around the feeder out of the windward

And snowy side of the feeder as they
Peck into the feeder and the two seem
To get along until an imposing
Tufted titmouse arrives on scene and

The chickadees are rousted and flee the
Feeder leaving the titmouse to his meal.

Dominance
is asserted
and established
instantaneously.

Lily the cat and my Mom are upstairs
When I arrive at the office which is
Inside of the house wherein I was raised
And I love my resonant solitude

Where the hum of the electricity
From the ancient freezer and the printer
And the bubbling of the aquarium
Engenders vibrations conducive for

Meditative writing with the words and
Phrases coalescing into meaning
Inspiring effervescence but then
Inevitably I hear the sound of

Descending footsteps portending a jolt
Disappointing me with interruption.

Impending
interruption
curdles into
a sour
sigh.

Sometimes I remember my old mentor
Cid Corman pronouncing that rhyme is dead
It's antiquated and lost its vigor
It's much better to speak freely instead
As language isn't so artificial
And resists being tied with pretty bows
The meaning with rhymes is superficial
Poetry becomes vainglorious pose
And rhyming sounds like pontification
The consequence of a fragile ego
It's better to go for self-negation
To exhibit oneself incognito
But is rhyme really dead — maybe not yet
I guess it all depends on a mindset.

It's not very hard to rhyme
And it doesn't take much time
Just type in a word
At RhymeZone.com
And find a rhyme anytime.

Our society is having a purge
Of the menace White Supremacy
So that justice will finally emerge
We have a problem with our history
Because we honor mendacious people
We must destroy statues and monuments
To create a benevolent sequel
The downtrodden will gain predominance
White women are not deserving of blame
But the white Christian men are the problem
We must make propitious use of shame
And follow the path of Joseph Stalin
Historical white men must disappear
And it's time to cancel William Shakespeare.

Shakespeare is just a big dope
Let's get ahold of a rope
We'll circle his head
So he can drop dead
And we can inspire hope.

In their wild beauty standing quietly
On this winter morning I am probing
For what do the trees mean to me today
As I see them through the periphery

Of the window as the rectangular
Window is a man-made fabrication
Worthy of appreciation but the
Naked trees upthrusting skyward are a

Testament of a cosmic genius as
All of the innumerable twigs are
Such delicate fingers and every bud
And leaf to come are eager tongues tasting

Absorbing the pulsation of the sun
Akin to my pulsating beating heart.

Asymmetrical trees
are equivalent in
creative force to
volcanoes.

The snow is descending in the finest
Of grains and I can imagine them to
Be like subatomic particles waving
Within a vast incomprehensible

Ocean of emanation shoreless and
Ceaseless and I recognize myself as
A node of consciousness capable of
Possessing only a glimpse of the truth

As I did nothing to deserve my heartbeat
My mobile body and my sensations
Of exploration and too often I
Am liable to squabble and jab at

Fellow human beings forgetful of
The redemption of curiosity.

I am curious
enough to grow
roots and probe
the sky with
questions.

The trees are dormant during the winter
But that doesn't mean they stand idly by
As roots are keeping them firmly in place
And they resonate mournfully with the

Wind and the blustery winter wind is
Sharp and stimulating so much better
Than the eternal silence of the moon
And I am grateful for the presence of

The trees for the shadows they lay upon
Fresh fallen snow and for the shelter they
Afford the crows chickadees cardinals
And the nuthatches as the winter birds

Are simpatico with the barren trees
Fitting together like yang beside ying.

Without meditative
awareness the trees
remain
invisible.

While waiting for a train in Amsterdam
On the ferry of the English Channel
Thinking about his poems on a tram
Visiting his gravesite in a chapel
I appreciated Shakespeare's sonnets
And adored his Elizabethan pomp
He was quite lovesick and I believed it
Inspiring an ethereal whomp
His verbiage is like thick molasses
With clever rhymes and opal metaphors
He gave vent to superlative passions
Not getting enough and wanting much more
Each of Shakespeare's sonnets is a puzzle
Lyrical exorbitant and subtle.

But I don't know why
anyone would rhyme like that
it's kind of crazy
this Houdini trick with words
is just piffle for the birds.

Sitting facing the window
Quiet like at a Zendo
A cardinal came
Smacked into the pane
And all I could say was "Oh!"

I am not a birder but do enjoy
Pointers passed on to me by Fran saying
Among winter birds in Minnesota
Are the smaller redpolls and house finches

That have similar streaky brown or gray
Markings over their white bellies and backs
And the males of the finches have splashes
Of red about their upper breast and the

Males of redpolls have pink-washed chests with a
Blotch of scarlet on their foreheads and I
Appreciate Fran's knowledge because I've
Never knowingly seen such birds and now

Because of Fran I am an older dog
With an epiphany ahead of me.

In every season
I have faith
there is a
revelation
to watch for.

Out of an empty sky the cardinal
Flew directly toward me and its motion
Instantaneously captivated
My attention and with a fleeting glimpse

I recognized the scarlet bird before
The disconcerting impact against the
Windowpane and he took the blow along
With my breath and flew off to the right

Which discombobulated my hunt for
Rhymes and I've done it also and I
Have walloped my head repeatedly and
There was a winter evening with an

Innocent stroll to a birthday party when
I smashed into and rattled a closed glass door.

I don't know about
the cardinal but for
me embarrassment
is worse than
shock.

Upon exiting my house and locking
The door I notice the caw of a crow
And look about for the bird toward the
Gigantic cottonwood on the corner

Of my property and I see the tree
Coated in a hoar frost and search and spot
The crow perching and I utter a "caw"
In turn and then another crow streaks in

The air to my right seizing my sight for
A moment and not dawdling I go in
The garage heave up the door drive out and
Get out of the car close the garage door

And perhaps another crow or the same
Crow flies by establishing his presence.

The six or seven
crows of the
neighborhood
seem to
recognize me.

By 1903 no one had done it
And I am old enough to remember
The jerky grainy black-and-white films of
Flailing flying contraptions as they launched

Off of piers and crashed into the water
Which I suppose is a propitious
Method for crashing without getting hurt
But the Wright Brothers accomplished the feat

Solving the problems of pitch roll and yaw
Engineering a motor with rotors
An elevator a rudder a right
Warp and curvature for a pair of wings

And at Kitty Hawk North Carolina
People did become flying animals.

It took modern nylon
and a lot more courage
to perfect
wingsuits.

In 2021 the latest
In a series of land rovers made it
To Mars arriving after rocketing
From Earth and traveling a distance of

292 million miles and
The appropriate name of the rover
Is "Perseverance" and this installment
Is unique in deploying over the

Martian surface the aptly entitled
"Ingenuity Helicopter" to
Preview the arid ground that the rover
Will encounter which is a tricky feat

Because the thin Martian atmosphere is
Only one percent of the Earth's air.

It's a challenge
to create enough
lift in the
unbreathable
Martian air.

The bone-chilling temperature on Mars
Is minus one hundred thirty degrees
Fahrenheit and it's a desert without
Oxygen and nothing is alive there

Yet very intelligent people are
Looking to colonize Mars after
Mankind has rendered Earth unlivable
Which is a queer eccentric opinion

Revealing exorbitant hubris
Concerning human capability
But also poisonous cynicism
About embryonic humanity

Because redemption is possible and
Our homely earth is all-encompassing.

How odd that
people can be
so clever
and stupid too.

While adoring the frozen winter trees
Absorbing their wild gesticulations
Appreciating the variety
And the delicacy of winter birds

It's easy to see their interwoven
Compatibility and it's fitting
To be happy about whatever it
Was that exploded 14 billion years

Ago and how marvelous it is to
Be awake and be attentive to the
Ongoing phantasmagoria of
Creation and I need as much of my

Intellect as I can muster but most
Of my adoration comes from my heart.

Who knows what
will emanate
from the
continuing
Big Bang?

I've taken to dangling a stone on a
Chain in front of my chakras to explore
What kind of energy my body is
Emanating at the moment and if

The stone goes around in clockwise circles
Then there's confirmation of a healthy
Equanimity of emotions and
Intellect but if the stone is hanging

Motionless there is evidence of a
Disturbance of the mind and the body
And then I hunt for the bodily source
And I'm finding that fear feels like a mass

Of concrete in my stomach and then it's
Good to consider what's causing the fear.

Thought
triggers
emotion
triggers
emanation.

I have been educated to know that
Every living being gives off subtle
Vibrations of energy even the
Happy woolly bear caterpillars that

Wiggle on the pavement before winter
And next year I will certainly dangle
A stone over them to see how they do
But anytime inside my home I may

Investigate the pitch and humming of
Kitcat only it's necessary to
Catch him unawares otherwise he will
Flip instantly onto his back and swipe

Lunge and bite the stone and then of course it
Is impossible to get a reading.

Kitcat is
always a
ragamuffin
rapscallion.

The amount of snow overnight was more
Than shovel work and it's better not to
Leave the snow blowers idle for too long
So I ran the machines and found the snow

Fluffy on top and greasy beneath and
It was an easy but messy chore in
Later February which signals that
Perhaps the coldest days of winter are

Over as we enter the pattern of
Thawing of snow during daylight and of
Freezing overnight as the trudge through the
Tundra of winter is lifting at last

And soon the brown grass will appear again
As the sunlight regains its potency.

Warming days
lull and tranquilize
but sloppy blizzards
are coming.

I saw outside of my window a pair
Of little gray birds with yellow beaks that
Hopped in the hedge before departing and
Several crows are flying together now

Above the trees and I'm remembering
A Buddhist saying about the empty
Space between things — the emptiness that binds
Everything together without a seam

Is the clarified mind without a thought
Like a mirror that of itself has no
Image contained within it but it does
Reflect all manifested liveliness

As everything I perceive does arise
Outside of and inside of my noggin.

I can't loiter
in clarity
because
the mind
cogitates.

There are things to do in a sudden thaw
Without a smidgeon of hesitation
It's like an ecclesiastical law
And to waste time is a violation
I race to the carwash and wait in line
Because the car is badly encrusted
As the snowplows spew a god-awful brine
And I refuse to let the car be rusted
So I will loiter with the radio
Snug like a bug in a rug in my car
Savoring the frothy sudsy gizmo
And afterward I can grin like a rock star
As life is so brief I do need to act
And enjoy more than my digestive tract.

I patiently wait my turn
Past the point of no return
I can't move an inch
I'm starting to itch
My heart's beginning to burn.

The blanket of snow won't be here for long
It's covered in rabbit and squirrel prints
As much milder days are coming along
But now there are innumerable glints
With sunlight sparking millions of crystals
Their fire is refracting in pinpoint jewels
Becoming sharp iridescent pixels
But quickly this snow will melt into pools
Clouds are making a high thin ceiling
Moving gradually within the sky
But even with the clouds it's revealing
The potency of light will multiply
Spring is approaching and the snow will go
And I will warm myself — like a tomato.

The red squirrel is busy
Running on top of the fence
He stops and he runs
He runs and he stops
Making perfect squirrel sense.

I do admit it isn't really fair
To compare my poems with what they did
It is easy now because of software
While they depended so much upon id
When weary I turn to a thesaurus
When rhyming I go to RhymeZone.com
To find a partner with "polymorphous"
And thereby poetizing with aplomb
But old-time poets relied on their heads
They couldn't surf the web for verbiage
They exhausted their gray matter instead
And they must have mustered so much courage
But I don't care and I am quite happy
That I can rhyme and make it sound snappy.

I come to my desk and sit
Hunting for a rhyme that fits
It's not for acclaim
It's only a game
Choosing a "banana split."

I do like my experiments with rhyme
It's not difficult and just takes practice
But I won't be doing it all of the time
To make it a habit would be madness
It's kind of crazy and not normal speech
It could easily be illogical
To rhyme formally is to sort of preach
And perhaps it is pathological
But just for a lark I would love to see
The president give special emphasis
And concoct a brand-new style by maybe
Rhyming the State of the Union Address
I would love to see that bunch of dummies
Sit and listen as it would be funny.

The president is stoic
He lives by the Potomac
Better than normal
Because he's formal
The president's heroic.

Rhyming is a Houdini trick with words
And there are combinations of words and
Thoughts that would never coalesce without
The impetus of making a rhyme and

I've discovered it is propitious
And wickedly decorous and pithy
To be slyly sarcastic while rhyming
Because creating a tune comports with

Humor but to rhyme and be sincere is
Tricky because in America now
Such formalized poetizing sounds quite
Odd and old-fashioned so striking the right

Tone becomes difficult within a form
That doesn't accommodate wiggle room.

Do you suppose
Pythagoras
could have
impressed by
rhyming
theorems?

You know Thag
It's all very fine
Your theorems
May be perfectly
Accurate
But they don't even rhyme!

I don't operate in isolation
As every action I take will spur a
Reaction as lately there's no problem
For me to fall asleep easily but

When I wake at 2 a.m. and am not
Depressed but my mind is buzzing with a
Self-satisfied happiness which isn't
Conducive for getting back to sleep I

Will spread my cushions upon the floor for
40 minutes of Zen meditation
But Kitcat expects that I am getting
Up and happy brushing time is coming

So he gallops noisily through all the
Rooms in the house and then he caterwauls.

I am seeking
disembodied repose
while Kitcat expects
brushing wrestling
slapping and biting.

I slip seamlessly from a vivid and
Poignant separation from my daughter
In a dream to wakefulness in bed and
I remember my son is living in

Alaska and we habitually
Don't communicate as I notice the
Pulsing of my heartbeat is prompting a
Throbbing sensation within my ears which

Reminds me of my intention to seek
For the locus of emotion within
My body and I think but am not sure
That sadness and grief are felt about my

Stomach as my stomach feels like a chunk
Of concrete which is a load to carry.

Every event of life
even the transition
from a dream is a
seamless continuous
reverberation.

This is an odd season of transition
From bitter cold to thawing and freezing
Overnight and on sunny days water
Will be running across the hilly streets

Of Stillwater down to the wide river
And every year I feel a lifting of
Burdens and a lightening of spirit
Very much like a liberation from

Despair but I have to remind myself
Of my locus in Minnesota where
The snow may melt precipitously to
Reveal the grass on the verging of a

Resurrection but within minutes the
Sky will change and dump a load of snow.

I steel myself
remembering from
November to April
every day is
February.

Around the trunks of my trees in my yard
The thawing of snow is expanding in
Wide circles revealing the brownish grass
And this pattern is repeated throughout

The neighborhood as if the roots of trees
Were warming the earth and melting the snow
Whereas the ground without roots beneath is
Covered in minutely pockmarked snow that

Bears evidence of thawing and freezing
And the wind has been blustery for the
Last few days causing the wild gesturing
Of the bare branches to violently

Sway in the air and I wonder whether
The trees are waking from winter slumber.

There is a new sparkle
in the morning sun
and its corona is
incandescent.

Each sheet of paper that bears evidence
Of my cogitation within the form of
My poetry that you are turning with
Your fingertips every single page that

Falls one upon another as you read
Expresses in the agreed upon forms
Of letters communicates with words and
Lines from me to you all of these pages

Originated in the liveliness
Of the trees the earth and the sun and the
Mixture of the earth air fire and water
Forming a mode of community through

Writing and reading transpiring through
Millennia of civilization.

All the permutations of
emotive
intellection
metamorphize on
wood pulp.

We were born and grew from the earth as a
Permutation of evolution and
Depended upon an interweaving
Of forces including the striking of

The earth by an asteroid prompting the
Extinction of the dinosaurs that made
Possible different forms of being
And the panorama of liveliness

Metamorphizes continually
Encompassing the fearsome certainty
Of other cataclysmic events and
We humans ourselves may even be the

Perpetrators — and even if we were
Would that fact be contrary to nature?

Nature is
incomprehensible
unpredictable
continuous
Wild.

Some of our befuddled scientists are
Supposing that within black holes that
Are scattered throughout the cosmos — and there
Maybe millions inside our Milky Way

Galaxy — there are singularities
Of infinite gravity where time is
Instantaneous and not linear
And the boundary between progressing

And extraordinary time shifts at the
Event horizon drawing everything
Inward with irresistible force and
What possible inference can be drawn

From the dawning of our comprehending
Consciousness of this arrangement of things?

I was nothing before
I became something
and will become nothing
again.

Questions for me percolate surrounding
The quantity and the quality of
Consciousness fixating upon whether
A protozoa has detectable

Selective aliveness and if so what would
Its experience be like and suppose
Assumed inanimate objects like the
Winter trees in Minnesota have an

Original form of thought about them
Responding to shifting temperature
And the orbital proximity of
The sun and if so then the vibrations

Blinking into and out of existence
Of waving quarks are infused with knowledge.

Things blink into and
out of existence from
nothing to something
to nothing.

The air is just about freezing and the
Precipitation is more of snow than
Sleet and the flakes are blowing sideway in
A vigorous wind and I can see the

Hedges and branches of trees are getting
Coated with the sticky kind of snow and
At times like this I wonder where do the
Delicate birds like the chickadee and

The titmouse go and what do they do for
Shelter as the crows and the gulls have more
Substance on their bones to handle this kind
Of moist and penetrating cold but the

Little birds are only skin feathers and
Bone and February can be nasty.

I imagine there are
the sides of hills and
walls or boulders
out of the way of
the blowing snow.

How does one reconcile with conflicting
Views of nature as the animals are
Gifted with claws and teeth and end up
Inside of each other's stomachs and we

Aren't much different with our warfare
Oppression and politics which devolve
Into all the subtle arts of deceit
And gossip and we apply our forms of

Industrial butcheries to species
Of animals for consumption and yet
We have a sensibility that points
To redemption-creating myths serving

To ennoble our perplexing struggles
Turning on courage and benevolence.

Is the warrior's
wrath both
bloody and
innocent?

Seeing the trees sway within a white sky
As the snow is curling sideways down with
A density that partly obscures the
Trees in the distance as the sky and snow

Are inseparable as the sky has
Descended to engulf within itself
All the moving trees of the neighborhood
As I am sheltered within an office and

Am observing warm and dry at my desk
And window typing words of description
Onto a broad computer screen of the
Same shade of white as the sky and snow and

The flakes of snow have become enormous
And every flake must be a touch of cold.

In the near distance I hear
the heavy metal blades
of snowplows scraping
snow off of the asphalt.

I can only see the barest outlines
Of winter trees within the blowing snow
But in fantasy I take possession
Of omnipotent vision instantly

Arriving upon any vantage of
Choosing and I would watch the crest of dawn
Spreading sunlight on the rotating Earth
And next I would take the best view of the

Swirling gaseous red spot of Jupiter
And then I would become a microscope
To observe the revolutions of the
Electrons of atoms and then I would

Launch myself to the edge of the cosmos
To know what is it expanding into.

Perhaps
motion
and
existence
are
inseparable.

According to the weather app on my
Cell phone the snow is supposed to stop in
45 minutes but I am looking
Out of the window now to verify

The cessation of snow and there high in
A tree a crow is perching and just now
I'm seeing another bird perhaps a
Sparrow flit and glide into the maple

And I don't know how the birds operate
But they have left shelter to do business
And I will take my cues from them and zip
Myself inside of a down jacket while

Wearing my big boots preparing to move
This sticky sloppy snow off the driveways.

Doing poetry first
and mindless
activity afterward
is harmonious.

Rhyming sonnets is an amusing game
As long as I admit they don't mean much
It's fun and maybe just a little lame
Even as the habit could be a crutch
Finding blustery words is a puzzle
Striking a pretentious poetic pose
Stirring up drama tempo and sizzle
And finishing with effortless repose
Surely the poet has sincerity
There's no purpose to writing otherwise
Just a useless verbal dexterity
But sometimes it's good to spring a surprise
I could put this sonnet on my tombstone
To inspire a laugh and not a moan.

Here lies Barry cold and dead
Without a thought in his head
He found clarity
And hilarity
With not a word left unsaid.

Snow will be melting in the next two weeks
All the walkways and roads will be a mess
And overnight so much water will freeze
So I walk with more than a little stress
As thin ice is almost invisible
So it's important to be clearheaded
Spotting a glint of ice is pivotal
Because I am not very hardheaded
And don't want to give my noggin a whack
It takes an instant of inattention
And more than my head could suffer a crack
I dread the tears of hyperextension
There are many perils that come with spring
And I don't want to see my legs upswing.

A moment's inattention
Means discombobulation
Involving a whack
Of a hard impact
And then incomprehension.

I am not deceived by appearances
I know all the snow is on the way out
But I don't forget my old grievances
I know what "spring melt" is really about
It is fabulous within a few days
Winter's accumulated snow will go
As the sun is marvelously ablaze
And the grass may even begin to grow
But it's a deception I've seen before
It seems the blizzards are finally gone
I don't have to wear big boots anymore
But it's a trick and I'm not a moron
It's a certainty in Minnesota
April blizzards are part of a quota.

The warmth is all very fine
And I enjoy the sunshine
It's no time for fun
Because we're not done
It will snow multiple times.

In the twilight zone between the ending
Of a dream and waking awareness I
Catch myself or maybe it is better
To say the apparition of ego

Is exposed in a poignant longing for
Things to be different than they are and
I see that the me who desires and
Is repulsed in dreams is identical

With the me of daylight activity
Except within dreams there is a freedom
From mundane circumstances giving space
For fantasy to play but at bottom

I realize I'm having a lot of
Fun wrestling with dissatisfaction.

I'd like to be more
explicit about
the details of the
dream but they slipped by
beyond my grasping.

I arrived home from the office to see
A pair of bald eagles in the branches
Of my cottonwood and as I approached
To get a better look one raised its wings

And it lifted off so impressing me
With the magnitude of its weight and size
In the slowness of its motion that I
Have never seen so close to home and

The neighbor said the excited crows of
The homely neighborhood grew quite upset
At being displaced from the prominence
Of the towering cottonwood by the

Unexpected presence of royalty
Based on superior size and talons.

Kitcat
in the house
won't meet
the eagle's
talons.

Writing sonnets loosey-goosey without
The task of rhyming is much easier
But in the play of rhyming the ends of
The lines I'm finding it's propitious

To be facetious and strike dramatic
Poetical poses variously
Smug or indignant as the poem turns
Which isn't a true personality

But piffle harmonious with rhyming
As I can't fathom being serious
And rhyming too because that would feel like
Wearing a colonial powdered wig

Which might have been OK for John Keats or
Robert Frost but seems obsolete to me.

But be alert
I also strike
piffling poetical poses
without rhyming.

In politics it is easy to lose
There is an art in prevaricating
It is beneficial to skew the news
So many events are irritating
The politicos know how to accuse
Shaping the narrative is important
It is a trick to confuse and abuse
Being honorable is impotent
To rise in the ranks they follow their cues
The system becomes a nasty machine
Originality they won't excuse
The exercise of force is often mean
Most Americans haven't got a clue
They are being deceived — I wish they knew.

He is honest he is bold
His virtue will not be sold
His integrity
And sincerity
Are a beauty to behold.

Give me the company of desperate
Drunks who are struggling to be sober
To drink is to die and they accept it
The forgetful bliss they had is over
The chaos they create is dangerous
They grieve their families and they know it
And then driving while drunk is treacherous
They have compulsion and can't control it
They need to talk to the people like them
They are confused and need to express it
They are terrified of the days to come
The urge is tempting but they repress it
And their loneliness is hard to fathom
It's necessary to hit rock bottom.

An alcoholic
has no control over how
much he drinks once he
starts again and no control
over the consequences.

The scorn he gets is understandable
There is not an easy explanation
The damage is incomprehensible
Apologies prompt exasperation
And the alcoholic is pathetic
Why on earth he can't stop is the question
And quite often he seems apathetic
He's not even open to suggestions
Or he's mournful and apologetic
And expresses the best of intentions
But it is hard to be sympathetic
He's not a person who learns his lessons
His drunken antics are deplorable
Living with him becomes unbearable.

He doesn't know why
he does what he does — even
the hangovers are
not enough to curtail an
inevitable binge.

So how does one help an alcoholic?
Relinquishing control is the first step
Repeating behavior is neurotic
And making excuses is a misstep
He has to hit bottom to get better
He has to suffer the consequences
The more pain he feels — so much the better
He needs to be stripped of his defenses
Coddling or soothing doesn't help him
Keep him from driving when drunk if you can
Call the police and let them arrest him
Let him suffer more pain than he can stand
His hitting rock bottom is essential
This isn't cruel — it is consequential.

There are circles of
sober alcoholics he
can join to gain the
communication and the
knowledge of recovery.

I understand them because I am one
And did get sober many years ago
What alcoholics do is what I've done
There are meetings and steps to undergo
Self-loathing isn't a permanent state
I've earned my freedom and my confidence
I learned how to pray and to meditate
And uncover the snares of consciousness
The hopeless desperation is a gift
A metamorphosis is possible
To perceive differently is a lift
To balance emotion is plausible
I don't live at all like I did before
And am not self-destructive anymore.

Thoughts and emotions
need not be weightier than
the clouds in the sky
if I can let go of them
then that is liberation.

The distant horizon is salmon pink
I have always loved watching the sunrise
Something about it forces me to think
It's more than a festival for my eyes
The trees are beautiful black silhouettes
Making a worthy foreground for the sky
There is a magic that we all possess
The power of consciousness in disguise
Intellect and emotions coalesce
Sensuous exploration clarifies
In meditation being may fluoresce
Disruptive circumstances harmonize
As the uprising sun may crystallize
There is a depth in peace to realize.

The moon is on
a different angle than
the spinning earth
as the moon shines before dawn
and after the sun rises.

I want to play and be spontaneous
I'm not aiming to be nasty or lie
I'd like to winnow what's extraneous
To empower me to hit the bullseye
My topics are contemporaneous
Some people are angry but I stand by
All kerfuffle is simultaneous
So many grievances do multiply
And opinions are miscellaneous
I am only an ordinary guy
But the sunrise is momentaneous
I'm not sure I'm making sense — but I try
And it is worthy to be conscientious
I'm not sure it's possible — I can't lie.

Dr. Seuss wrote children's books
He wrote funny rhyming hooks
Thing One and Thing Two
They matter to you
We all love his storybooks.

The trick in life is to be lovable
The trap to avoid is rigidity
Love is happiness love is flammable
It consumes the heart with rapidity
It's most helpful to be adaptable
Be like water possess fluidity
No one's perfect we all are fallible
To condemn yourself is stupidity
And to make mistakes is acceptable
Meditation offers lucidity
So much of the world can be magical
Be enlightened with pellucidity
There's more to life than being logical
Find wisdom in the mythological.

I start my day with my cat
And every morning we chat
We wrestle and fight
And he tries to bite
We have a playful combat.

I don't want to be ceremonial
I'd like to think I have sincerity
I favor words that are colloquial
Without descending to vulgarity
It's not hard to be sanctimonial
With a scornful familiarity
But it's more playful to be jovial
Being deceitful is barbarity
To utter jargon would be provincial
I want joyful conviviality
The meaning should be unmistakable
A lightning bolt comes from temerity
With an added touch of hilarity.

God help me I'm liking it
Looking for the rhymes that fit
I sit on my butt
And create rut
Being a silly nitwit.

The patter of words is delectable
And the lines are a pleasure to compose
The easier words are more digestible
And then they may topple like dominoes
Sometimes my manner is questionable
Being mischievous I won't foreclose
A sly subtlety is detectable
As every new line will superimpose
It is horrid to be predictable
I keep in my pocket a yellow rose
Oh my habits are uncorrectable
I am a rascal right down to my toes
I am trying to be respectable
But the rhyming is too obsessional.

So often I am doing it
Can't really excuse it
It's a waste of time
Just trying to rhyme
Pretty soon I will stop it.

Each of my poems is a flirtation
In a way I'm saying "come play with me"
You don't have to — there's no obligation
But playing with words is my specialty
You don't need crafty sophistication
Poetry can be light and feathery
I don't harbor any expectations
But how many ways can we say "Whoopee"?
I won't pronounce fussy declarations
I won't be a scary mournful banshee
Having fun needs no justification
We can frolic like golden bumblebees
The words are more than mere decoration
They may inspire your liberation.

Let's try for simplicity
With happy complicity
We don't need bother
We won't use blather
We can have felicity.

The air is alive with the presence and
The songs of birds again in the light of
The rising sun at Pioneer Park as
I see an orange tanager in the

Oak and hear the irrepressible cheers
Of house finches and a squadron of geese
And of trumpeter swans make their arrow
Formations in the sky and the crows are

Busy communicating while flying
Continuously between the trees and
I see a crow carrying twigs in its
Beak as drops of melting snow are falling

Steadily from the eaves of the wooden
Shelter making spring music on concrete.

We group of happy
ex-drunks gather in the park
conversing about
sobriety while bingeing
on spring optimism.

It's common among problem drinkers to
Worry after having a dream wherein
The aspirant for sobriety has
Failed and given in to temptation and

Is stupefied drunk again and burdened
With a dump-truck load of shame and saddened
With the perplexity of whether to
Honestly admit his relapse to his

Faithful companions or to make the lapse
A secret and silently carry the
Guilt but upon awakening relief
Is palpable as the experience

Was only a nighttime fantasy and
Grateful redemption arrives with the sun.

A drinking dream is
a propitious sign of
earnest effort as
it only occurs when the
drunk has determinedly quit.

It's also common among us problem
Drinkers amidst our inebriation
To squirrel away hidden bottles of
Booze in propitious places above

Door frames or in our attics and basements
Or in a thousand other sly spaces
Escaping the notice of a spouse and
After the threshold of sobriety

Is crossed many containers of liquid
Joy are forgotten like landmines waiting
For discovery and I knew a guy
Who put in fences and he littered the

Countryside with hidden bottles inside
Of culverts underneath the lonely roads.

Drunken fools
really are similar
to squirrels
hiding
acorns.

It's difficult now and I don't know why
I'm much more frantic than I want to be
There is frustration but I will get by
Usually I have more energy
That is not true and I'd rather not lie
I am just not seizing my synergy
I've become an inarticulate guy
And not the poet that I'd like to be
My mind is awake but it won't comply
If the words don't flow then I'm not happy
I will calm myself and detoxify
And God keep me from becoming sloppy
I really have to try and simplify
It is my only chance to clarify.

Morning is my apogee
Morning is my jubilee
I rise with the sun
And then I have fun
Morning is my energy.

You don't have the time to fritter away
Don't allow cogitation to stultify
You must gather yourself and seize the day
You can't let your synapses ossify
The world's a festival — go out and play
Don't let your knees and elbows calcify
You may still vacation in Paraguay
Think of all the whimsy to gratify
Excite your companions host a soirée
Contact an old friend and reunify
You might even be a little risqué
You can't let epiphanies pass you by
Liberate anxiety with reggae
Enjoy Hemingway with café au lait.

Don't be sorry don't be blue
Get over that stomach flu
Life is savory
It's not slavery
Take a trip to Katmandu.

You are lucky you aren't a crustacean
Excuse me I don't mean to speechify
You need not listen to my dictation
Being human — what does that signify?
I say it's a cause for celebration
We have both arms and legs — do you know why?
I really enjoy my ambulation
And wouldn't want to be a tsetse fly
That would be such a humiliation
I can do subtractions and multiply
And contribute to civilization
I can classify and personify
Having fingers for manipulation
And a big brain for specification.

Doggerel isn't easy
As it needs to be breezy
It has to be fun
And turn on a pun
Even if it is cheesy.

The air isn't cold but is quite chilly
The overcast sky is a gloomy gray
But I am happy and even silly
I'm pretty sure it's going to rain all day
The snow is mostly gone and there's the grass
The frost is leaving and the soil is moist
Sure it's messy now but the rain will pass
Every year at this time I do rejoice
This is different than a winter day
The air is very damp and quite misty
The dry lip-splitting air has passed away
This kind of air makes metal things rusty
I know there will be snowy days to come
But now I see no reason to be glum.

The tumultuous
howling wind of the last few
days must have roused the
roots of the trees from slumber
to take minerals again.

I confess to a little negligence
I am supposed to be reading the news
But it's an insult to intelligence
And every day it's just a nasty ooze
It's full of opinion that I don't trust
Reporters are condescending and smug
Topics they cover are meant to disgust
But the overall impact makes me shrug
I'm sure the news is manipulative
News people present slanted opinions
They think their views are authoritative
They want to foist important decisions
Reading the news is a predicament
I take it in selective increments.

I like writing poetry
It's like psychotherapy
I do not scowl
I do not growl
Usually I'm happy.

I learn a lot from my metal dumbbell
It just lies on the floor so patiently
But it has the oomph to make me humble
And I can't lift it with complacency
As it weighs exactly 100 pounds
It takes my focus and it makes me strain
And I do struggle with the ups and downs
And the effort even squeezes my brain
I do have a fear of letting it go
Because my wrists aren't quite sturdy enough
I am terrified of smashing a toe
But absolutely I'm not giving up
Usually it's a hunk of metal
But its latent force is elemental.

It's not lovely it's not art
Doesn't really warm my heart
And my dumbbell
Doesn't ever smell
Though it often makes me fart.

To any amount determinable
Without any perception deleted
Even though perhaps unmanageable
Maybe so unusually gifted
Not excluding many obtrusive things
Including the imperceptibly small
Involving the physics theories of strings
Wanting it too much creates a pitfall
Sometimes an unavoidable nuisance
Resonating in a temple bell's gong
Encompassing desperate truculence
Also the unjustifiably wrong
You see enlightenment is everything
In partnership with a pregnant nothing.

It's not me who is
responsible for this
poem as I laid
my head upon my pillow
and words came from somewhere else.

Suddenly
gloom
intensifies
with
impending
rain.

—*Tekkan*

Everyday Mind XX

Bare
branches
sway in the
wind — the
sun
dazzles.

The barren trees are swaying in the breeze
The grass is dry but it's not growing yet
It's warm today but it's kind of a tease
Spring is coming but it isn't here yet
Snow is approaching but there won't be much
There's no denying the sun's new dazzle
And snow will fall but I'm not caring much
As winter's grasp is becoming feeble
I'm looking forward to the bright fresh leaves
To the budding of the apple blossoms
I want to hear the wind tossing the leaves
I love crabapple and cherry blossoms
And it won't be long before we hear the frogs
The tree the chorus and the peeper frogs.

Spring leaves
in breezes
tumble
swell
soothe.

This could be a day in February
As it snowed last night and the sky is white
But the snow is only temporary
And most of it will be gone by tonight
I'm taking the time to enjoy the snow
As if I had never seen it before
Very soon the grass will begin to grow
And it won't be bitter cold anymore
The weight of winter is dissipating
I can feel a spring moisture in the air
Bright days are coming — I don't mind waiting
Gloom may be lingering but I don't care
So many winters have come and passed by
But I never tire of watching the sky.

Winter dissipating
river ice dissolving
birds and trees
grass and leaves
soon titillating.

My blackened toenails needed a year to
Grow out enough for me to clip off the
Damage that resulted from wearing shoes
The pinched my toes and it won't happen again

And I will traverse the countryside with
Jason again like we did last year and
He will take enormous bounding strides
At an arduous pace and I will struggle

To keep up and we will explore
Springtime resurrection again and
He will use ecological wisdom
To expose my ignorance and explode

My misapprehensions and I will be
Exhausted afterwards but satisfied.

And my toenails
afterwards will
remain pink and
pristine inside of
better shoes.

Jason sees a gaggle of geese and swans
Flying together in one formation
Jason understands the geese and the swans
Not surprised by their cooperation
He strides through William O'Brien State Park
And it's exhausting for me to keep up
He points out the Neolithic landmarks
After eleven miles he speeds up
He tells me about the various trees
He sees flowers that don't look like flowers
He has a mastery of the species
As I stride stomp and struggle for hours
Afterwards I know much more than I did
And my feet are aching and I'm done in.

For Jason every
season is not merely a
repetition of
of previous seasons but
a new origination.

We are lucky to find the ones in our
Lives who hear our words and intentions who
Have the persistence to see the layers
Of complexity and contradictions

And foibles and who accept and love us
With whom we in our turn may practice the
Skills of listening and of accepting
Our conflicting opinions and habits

Without recourse to coercive measures
As getting along harmoniously
Is a trick of compromise of letting
Go of expectations because the turns

Of circumstances will be jarring and
A loving partner is invaluable.

Whatever I think
will happen
probably won't
happen like that.

I didn't see the end coming and I'm
Sad we aren't a match but I'm grateful for
The conversation we shared drawing out
The pivotal experiences of

Our lives that made us the people we are
Today and I won't forget your kindness
And your probing intelligence — but you
Befuddled me by breaking it off so

Suddenly — and now you are teaching me
The lesson of how to let go without
Recrimination as I aspire
To be as light as a feather with the

People I love allowing emotions
To simmer freely and then to settle.

Letting emotions
come and go
without having to
figure them out
is excellent practice.

Taking a walk around a lake I see
The cattails along the shore that prospered
Last summer but now they're dried and lifeless
And I wonder how is it that these dead

Stalks will be removed and replaced by a
New generation as nature has a
Way of continuing and I feel and
Listen to the wind wrapping about me

And into my ears communicating
A sharp and eerie force of nature that
Chafes and chills as I encounter that which
Disintegrates forms and yet somehow makes

Possible the arising of other
Forms that flourish under a summer sun.

How shall I
characterize the wind —
indifferent
mournful
joyful?

There is so much happening when I step
Outside of my house with not a cloud in
The sky as the chilly air is like a
Moist tonic of spring liveliness bracing

And intoxicating and the air is
Filled with what seems celebratory
Birdsong of which I can identify
The irrepressible house finches but

There is a medley unknown to me
As the urgency and boisterous tunes
Of the birds overwhelm the gentle breeze
As the birds are invisible perching

In innumerable branches but their
Presence is impossible to ignore.

Is the urgency of
morning birdsong
of celebration or of
competition?

The male birds are moved in the morning to
Make their presence known to establish their
Territories and find mates which is an
Aggressive urgency that appears like

Celebration but is an assertion
Of strength and will as the primacy of
Mating fills these delicate creatures of
Feathers and bones living within their scope

Of a cosmos inaccessible to
Me but I have the detached pleasure of
Listening and of seeing the array
Of their plumage in happenstance glimpses

As I go about my business immersed
Within a world of conflicted thinking.

Open sky
swaying branches
singing birds are
a weaving of
cosmic becoming.

Walking away from another woman
After six months of companionship is
Not so easy as her manner of thought
And being were becoming enfolded

Within mine but the sudden break also came
With a sense of relief as I knew we
Were compatible in certain ways
And not so much in other ways and time

Was necessary to weigh whether
We could be together and my mind is
Recalling the words of encouraging
Enthusiasm we shared but also

The misgivings and reservations I
Felt that I suspect she was aware of.

Finding durable
compatibility
between complicated
singles is
tricky.

The crow is taken by the wind and blown
Across the sky tilting its wings letting
The forceful current of air overwhelm
Its intended direction pushed aside

From where it was going and it doesn't
Resist the wind but goes along with it
In harmony as the branches of the
Trees of the neighborhood are all swaying

Continuously in a spring uproar
As the first budding of the new leaves is
Becoming visible reviving a
Pattern of resurrection that I am

Familiar with but for the passing crow
Every spring must be a revelation.

I don't know where
the crow went as
it probably perched
in a tree within its
territory.

Outside of my portal of a window
Where I sit and type my poems as I'm
Watching the world there is a cottonwood
Tossing within a wind as a crow is

Perching on a branch bobbing its head and
Splaying and folding its tail feathers and
Flapping its wings and then it departs and
As I'm watching higher up several

Crows are determinedly forcing their way
Against the wind and a single crow is
Following behind and I'm reminded
Of the arrowhead formations of the

Geese that are evolved to efficiently
Cut through air by the thousands of miles.

The crows haven't
formed themselves
for the long haul of
migration — they
are homebodies.

On the thresholds of the Shinto shrines in
Japan there are standing tori gates which
Are the barest of structures comprising
Only two vertical posts — through which the

People enter the shrines — that are topped by
Two horizontal beams and the passage
Of the gates symbolizes the leaving
Behind of the ordinary and the

Entering of the sacred precinct of
The shrines and the gates are said to be the
Abodes of the birds and because I'm not
Japanese I may mistake their meaning

But I adore the idea that one
May take a step and enter into peace.

The gates are painted
vermilion a shade
of bright
loveliness.

I am a believer in the troughs and
Crests of life having experienced the
Intimacy and the solicitude
Of love for a time which I assumed would

Continue indefinitely and now
I know how it feels to have love withdrawn
Suddenly and seemingly without a
Reason and there's anger and hurt and a

Compulsion to figure out what happened
But really there's nothing to do but to
Receive the disorientation of
A loss which is a trough on the way to

Becoming a crest while accepting the
Traumatic quality of emotion.

Each personality
leaves ripples
merging into
incessant
undulation.

I went to match.com and renewed my
Membership and updated my profile
With a suggestion that women of a
Political persuasion probably

Wouldn't work for me because it's a fact
Today society is polarized
Into factions and even with people
Who don't like politics and who don't watch

The news their opinions are already
Cast in concrete and differing thought may
Spark a hair-trigger reaction maybe
Not today but eventually so

With bruising experience I've learned to
Sidestep trouble with preemptive phrasing.

Mating is
much less
complicated
for the birds.

The tripwires crossing society are in
Flux as I got a call from a retired
Coal miner in Ohio in response
To a sales letter I sent inviting

Subscriptions to a publication that
I operate and in conversation
He revealed divisions between the
Union leadership and the miners and

He talked about dishonesty and the
Difficulty of separating the
Facts from rhetoric and promises made
And based on a similarity of

Of opinion we found agreement that
The direction of the nation is bad.

No matter where
a person stands
the tripwires of
politics are
dangerous.

In the land of the Wiener schnitzel this
Animal was bred for hunting badgers
In dens so it has muscled front legs with
Sharp claws for digging in the earth and it

Is doggedly determined on a hunt
Possessing a pointy nose and sharp teeth
A barrel chest with plenty of heart for
A fight and it has a resonant bark

With soulful eyes and facial expressions
With a proud and a confident carriage
Being brave to the point of recklessness
And rumbustiously adorable but

The wiener dog is wary and jealous
So be careful because he may bite you.

The dachshund has
intelligent eyes
pleading for table scraps
which it shouldn't get
lest it become fat.

The wiener dog has pomp and dignity
It's not concerned about your opinion
In its own way it displays symmetry
It's not a dog of easy submission
The dachshund is intelligent and bold
Bred by the Germans for hunting badgers
Its trotting style is a sight to behold
And the dog has a mouth full of daggers
It is long of body and short of leg
The carriage of its head shows confidence
With strangers it may be a powder keg
It has an appetite that's bottomless
And the dog may beg with very sad eyes
But tossing it table scraps is unwise.

The wiener dog is sporty
The wiener dog is snippy
its trotting along
is worthy of song
The wiener dog is perky.

Maybe it's better to be ignorant
And ignore political opinion
To slide by and become indifferent
And avoid the difficult decisions
But I'm not passive and I care too much
That politics today is dangerous
I'd like to discourse with a feather's touch
But so many topics are treacherous
We are spoon-fed nonstop accusation
Politicos purposely polarize
They profit from flammable gyrations
They hone their messages to demonize
The media is used to hypnotize
With the cruel intention to brutalize.

Lawyers and judges
law enforcement bureaucrats
the educators
and the media people
are all bitter partisans.

The issues are like Russian nesting dolls
Each of the dolls appears differently
A difference in knowledge makes a wall
Without knowledge there is no sympathy
The biggest doll is the news narrative
Partisan journalism isn't true
News is emotional and addictive
There is much dishonesty to sort through
Each doll presents greater complexity
The range of opinion is tremendous
Involving the context and history
And a lively debate could be endless
But the smallest doll is about power
And the truth about politics is sour.

Rules for Radicals
by Saul Alinsky and
The Prince
by Machiavelli
reveal the various tricks.

What do we mean when we say "consciousness"?
Does it include what we do while sleeping?
Is it just a measure of thoughtfulness?
Does everything have it if it's living?
I look at turkey vultures and eagles
Watching how they drift and soar with the wind
I listen to the mournful calls of gulls
Are they outside or inside of my mind?
I do some things of which I'm not aware
I am breathing lungs and beating a heart
Circulating blood and growing my hair
Am I one with the earth or set apart?
There is the weightiness of emotions
As imponderable as the oceans.

Do I separate
what happens
from how I respond?

The conference in Dallas launches on a
Friday evening with a cocktail hour which
Is challenging for me because I am
A stranger to everyone and I am

Compelled with the task of imposing
And introducing myself to people
Who know each other and who are engaged
In coteries of conversation as

They stand imbibing exhilarating
Drinks sporting their prestigious status and
Exchanging clubby insider's language
And awkwardly I do barge into a

Threesome smiling and showing off my teeth
Doing my best to be intelligent.

Polite society
is loaded with
tricks of
inclusion and
exclusion.

I heard a computer engineer talk
To a neurobiologist about
Artificial Intelligence and of
The potential dangers of runaway

Mechanical calculations made by
Hyperactive computers engendered
By humans that could only be held in
Check by competing platforms of "A. I."

Wherein if one system does establish
Preeminence then that entity would
Eliminate all competitors and
Lead to the subjugation of or the

Extinction of humanity which does
Imply that predation is foreordained.

The engineer seems
an updated version
of Dr. Frankenstein
touting the latest
silicon monster.

On Sunday morning the desk clerk called a
Taxi to the airport for me and on
His arrival the driver took my bag
And swung it into the trunk and on the

Ride he said his name was Sam and that
He missed driving in New York City and
He asked if I heard the speech from the
Rich man last night and I didn't know who

He was referring to and he said that
The Dallas airport is the only one
That charges taxis coming and going
And when we arrived the meter was on

Fifty dollars but he mumbled something
And then he charged me one hundred dollars.

I was caught off guard but I
have his name and cab number
and will claw back a refund
from Yellow Cab and
withdraw the tip.

A surge of power presses my body
As the engines roar along the runway
Speed is intensifying mightily
As the weight of my body falls away
As the airliner's wheels are lifting off
A thrust of power is precipitous
The plane is ascending steeply aloft
The engine's roaring is continuous
Pressure on my ears is making them pop
Something feels different but I'm not sure what
I'm feeling the blood in my temples throb
My seatbelt is locked and I'm staying put
The view from the window is amazing
The earth far below the clouds is moving.

Stuck in my seat
I'm reading a novel
waiting patiently
for a bottle of water
almonds and a biscuit.

The wind is taking me in sudden bursts
Testing the balance of the bicycle
It comes in roaring overwhelming spurts
But I can make it more manageable
I have to tame my appetite for speed
Because the wind is much stronger than me
Setting a gentle pace is what I need
The motion is easy and I'm carefree
It's exciting with the wind at my back
Now I'm speeding as fast as a greyhound
The time passes quickly and I lose track
My animal spirit is quite unbound
Spring is coming and the trees are budding
Today is joyous — the sunlight stunning.

The rippling river
far below the bridge
reflects sky and clouds —
the wind batters me
and the gulls.

I am sitting at a window and a
Desk watching the world parade by at
A pace that isn't lackadaisical
Or hurried seeing a puff of a cloud

Transforming in a northwesterly wind
When I see on the hedge four feet away
The birds that Fran had told me about that
I had never knowingly seen — redpolls —

And there is a male with splashes of red
About its chest and head and a female
Turning their heads and moving in jerky
Motions and I could have been lost thinking

About the taxi driver who tried to
Cheat me but instead I see the birds.

Beyond thought the
world is parading
neither rushed nor
lackadaisical.

Fran pointed out the difference between
The flights of turkey vultures and eagles
As the gliding of the wings of eagles
Is flat and the wings of the vultures have

More of a V shape and just a few words
Has improved my clarity of view and
Though the added insight doesn't give me
An ounce of leverage over people

It does impart a touch of pleasure as
I can see a little better into
The ceaseless parading of the earth as
Branches with emerging buds are swaying

In blusters and a few clouds are drifting
Southward at a pace that isn't harried.

The earth is wiggly
within a procession
of cyclical emergence
and disappearance.

It's easy to miss how lucky we are
Just stare at the news to become depressed
The propaganda they push is bizarre
Consume too much and you will be confused
Indulging anger is a sad mistake
I know because I've done it quite often
Resentment produces only heartache
I'd rather my emotions be softened
There is a vast world beyond my thinking
Occasionally I holiday there
Spring is coming and the trees are waking
And jubilant birdsong is in the air
Thought follows thought follows thought —
It's so easy to get tied up in knots.

Breath follows
breath follows
breath — it's
a better rhythm
to attend to.

It's April 1st and I'm feeling lazy
The snow is all gone and the sky is blue
Playing with words is a little crazy
I am sure there's something better to do
It's too chilly to ride my bicycle
I'm at my desk looking out my window
Just doing nothing isn't radical
It is better than playing pachinko
Oh well I lost a girlfriend poor poor me
I am just too weary to change her mind
There are advantages to being free
I can play with words if I'm so inclined
There are parts of me I don't want to change
So it's a better deal to disengage.

I am lackadaisical
with love drifting along
listening to bird song
too lazy to
move.

We ex-drunks meet in the park for our talk
Leveraging our sobriety while
Watching the sun rising and the vultures
Circling in the air as I stand freezing

My ears realizing sometimes it takes
More than a little adversity to
Summon the willingness to overcome
Self-pity and resentment coming so

Easily and afterward I rush home to
Fill my two containers with coffee and
I drive to the office preparing to
Drop into my chair eager to futz with

Words but then I realize that my phone
Is charging at home and that I need it.

Mornings are so
intoxicating that
sometimes details
escape me.

A scrap of information confided
Casually by a friend altered my
Everyday mind and now I am seeing
Differently what I had misperceived

Repeatedly so I am grateful to
Fran who revealed that they aren't eagles
But turkey vultures effortlessly and
Continuously singly or in wakes that

Are exploiting the thermal currents of
Air and without the circling of the birds
The quality of the restless air would
Be invisible and so I wonder

What else is eluding me — what else is
Over the horizon of my knowing.

I am only
sixty-three years old
and have plenty
of time left.

Let's have fun with innocent malaprops
I want to dance with you the flamingo
Let's have popcorn and watch an agitprop
A most lovely bird is the flamenco
The English language is full of riddles
The same vowels are spelled so differently
My handwriting is an awful scribble
I'm not capable of calligraphy
As I kid I was inarticulate
No one's ideal of virtuosity
I wasn't suspected of intelligence
And had not a hint of verbosity
But now I am old and full of whimsy
Don't give a damn — and my ego's flimsy.

Trouble comes from
being serious —
nonsense is
easy.

I would like my mind to be like a bowl
And to accept with grace phenomenon
To be happy to observe a redpoll
Or whatever birds I happen upon
But I get bogged down with controversy
And there is no end of trouble and strife
A head full of resentments is messy
Like cutting off toes with a butcher knife
Trying to make sense is a loser's game
If I try too hard I'm certain to fail
There is always someone that I can blame
With plenty of meatheads to put in jail
Writing doggerel is a saving grace
Much better than packing a can of mace.

There are always
birds flitting by
fitting in my
brain bowl
perfectly.

Whoever said that nonsense was easy?
All sensibility is pushed aside
I try to be just a little crazy
And assert a posture that's quite cockeyed
I may be lusty and may be lazy
Neither fastidious nor dignified
When learning the rules I may be hazy
Of formalities I am horrified
I'd like to see an African daisy
As long as I'm sure it is bonafide
And I'd love to savor bouillabaisse
But green pea soup I really can't abide
I like to loiter and come in with the tide
Don't have expectations — I may backslide.

This rhyming
business is just
abysmal
fizzle and
piffle.

There are Zen koans in which the monks are
Challenged to take Mount Fuji out of a
Pill box or to pull the four divisions
Of Tokyo out of a sleeve of a

Kimono and I don't pretend to know
The answer to these riddles that the monks
Grappled with to the point of despair but
As I look out of the window seeing

The same trees that are here day after day
And feel the upholding support that the
Chair is giving me I make a bubble
Of warm oxygen about myself and

Notice the gravitational tug of
The event horizon of a black hole.

Holding a closed fist
and persuading a child
there's something inside —
such are the riddles of
Zen.

The absence of a girlfriend is tricky
I do appreciate conversation
My expectations aren't a bit picky
And splitting up has brought a deflation
But I'm not unhappy to be alone
Now I don't have to match her schedule
I'm not spending so much time on the phone
Twining my thoughts with hers was typical
It's true I need others to be healthy
I do want a person to bounce off of
Do I want to be controlled? Not really
I'll find another way of doing love
My home is like a Zen monastery
Where probing my thought is salutary.

Nonsensical
utterance with
Kitcat keeps the
house lively.

The wiener dog is a noble creature
He doesn't care that his legs are so short
For self-confidence he is my teacher
His comportment upon the earth is stout
Looking at him you would think that he "yips"
But instead he has a mighty dog's bark
With his barrel chest he can let 'er rip
And he also has the teeth of a shark
It's said he is a good family dog
As he begs at dinner for table scraps
With such sad eyes he starts a dialogue
But his persuasive eyes are only traps
You shouldn't give in because he'll get fat
So please don't be responsible for that.

The unselfconscious
trotting gait of
the wiener dog
bespeaks dignity.

Animals are lucky that they don't think
They don't cultivate weighty opinions
Their vision and impulses are in sync
They don't agonize over decisions
They're not wasting any time on mirrors
They couldn't care less about self-image
They don't do their own accounting figures
They're not scornful — they don't do patronage
A hippo is ugly but doesn't care
Elephants are wise but they don't worry
A deer endures losses but doesn't swear
An aging lion doesn't feel sorry
Humans are burdened with conflicting thoughts
We tie ourselves in complicated knots.

But there's poignancy
and redemption in
simplifying
burdened
thought.

Seeds of the poem are in the first line
Only a hint will make a beginning
And fibrous roots become curious twine
This open moment is worth exploring
Ideas may be lively and playful
Syllables take on rhythm and meaning
My inspiration tends to be grateful
Don't know what I am anticipating
Might I journey in any direction?
Line after line compels a commitment
I like the subtlety of inflection
Looking back I can see I'm consistent
Sincerity of purpose will evoke
An acorn creates a mighty bur oak.

I could have been
a resentful drunk —
today I cultivate
hints of
possibility.

Buds of the trees are irrepressible
Sunlight is becoming solicitous
This lively season is unquenchable
But I do feel a little wistfulness
Air in spring is quite intoxicating
I won't allow myself to be inside
Is it my heart or the sun pulsating?
Though after a while I am getting fried
As I have lived though many springs before
And each one appears a resurrection
But I am really not young anymore
And can't stop my having circumspection
The spring is always extrasensory
And I carry a weight of memory.

Apple blooms are
on the way while the
intimacy I've known
has gone away.

There is a chemistry between people
An ease of comfort or nervous tension
As our experience isn't equal
Which affects our manner of expression
There are two women of my acquaintance
With each one I behave differently
With one I exhibit loving patience
With the other verbal dexterity
Each one elicits a version of me
And with both I'm being true to myself
I am behaving spontaneously
They are also genuinely themselves
Without you I don't know who I could be
I discover you and you unfold me.

Alone with my
thoughts so much
of my thinking is
conversation
reverberating.

Rhyming is a game so don't expect much
It's not really serious but it's fun
I want to imitate a feather's touch
Before you notice the poem is done
Just being sensible can be messy
What can I do with galloping nonsense?
And can I make my proofreaders fussy?
Correcting faulty grammar can be tense
Sometimes I think that I'm wasting my time
There are productive chores to be doing
I could be putting on a pantomime
Then I wouldn't have to write anything
But rhyming and fooling can be handy
Reducing today to cotton candy.

It's tricky to make a pun
Only for a bit of fun
Ignoring my work
And going berserk
And suddenly I am done.

It's a shame that I have to be wary
That often it's better to be quiet
Politics these days has gotten scary
And it's necessary to be private
I thrive on intellectual questions
I like to parse the various issues
But want to do it without aggression
The need for honest debate continues
But I've never seen such intolerance
It's easy to be smeared as a "hater"
But it's vile a mass of incoherence
With worse consequences coming later
The media is revolutionized
Public discussions have been brutalized.

I'd like to think
friendships are immune
to political pressures
but it's better not to
test.

It is clever to make accusations
Hurling narratives of collective guilt
It's a crafty form of misdirection
As the opposition cowers and wilts
Groups of people are said to be hateful
Based on perceptions of race or gender
While the accusers themselves are spiteful
And guilty of what they say of others
Trained activists are making the charges
Accusing innocent working people
The supposed solutions are mirages
The hatred created may be lethal
It is a dirty dishonest system
Persuading people that they are victims.

Leverage comes from
accusing the innocent
and directing
an army of
angry victims.

America is in turmoil today
Even in the midst of prosperity
Our trust in each other is giving way
We don't appreciate our luxuries
And we are shredding our institutions
Cops are suspects of criminal intent
Celebrities call for prosecution
There are surging rages of discontent
Controversies are splintering our schools
Is America an evil nation?
We can't agree on societal rules
The news is full of rabid gyrations
And public discourse dispenses venom
Every news cycle is now a weapon.

Disconnecting from
the news isn't a
protection from
societal drift.

Resentment is a terrible master
Inspiring malignant obsessions
An attractive trick for news broadcasters
Spurring the viewers' latent aggressions
The news depicts the plight of victimhood
Seizing events and forming narratives
But pivotal details aren't understood
Shaping opinion is imperative
Scorn is focused on the perpetrators
Those whom the media want to destroy
Reporters assume the role of saviors
Directing hate is a lucrative ploy
Humans have an appetite for anger
It seems an unappeasable hunger.

Am I not as guilty
as those whom I
accuse? Escaping
resentment is
tricky.

Life doesn't fit in simple narratives
Choices are a maze of complexity
It's not helpful to be comparative
Much better to consider empathy
Resentment is a terrible poison
It's not worth the self-consuming fury
Even for justifiable reasons
It makes all other emotions heavy
But the pain of resentment helped me change
I had to learn the art of letting go
Mistrusting my own thoughts at first was strange
I had to cultivate a faith and grow
I suffered a measure of frustration
Enough to desire liberation.

Resenting is like
setting my own house
on fire and
refusing to
escape.

A steady rain has dominated for
The last several days with the persisting
Sunlight being filtered through the gloom of
Dark gray clouds but I can't help rejoicing

Because the grass is greening with new growth
As the frost is gone and the soil is moist
And I've washed and put away my winter
Fleeces and the branches of the trees that

I've watched through the bitter cold are budding
With incipient leaves and the croaking
Of frogs is mixing with the sounds of the
Birds and yes there are moments when the light

Of day suddenly dims with the threat of
Impending rain but this is all joyous.

The complexity
of human entanglements
vanishes once the
prospect of pedaling on
my bicycle returns.

We hadn't seen Steve since the beginning
Of the pandemic a year ago but
He showed at the park for our meeting as
Curmudgeonly as usual with more

Gray hair than before and looking worn by
The separation imposed by the fear of
Catching the virus which has lifted from
Him as he is vaccinated now and

Is reclaiming his place among us in his
Turn speaking honestly and assessing
How he's doing remarking that it seems
Like years have passed but then as we regain

Familiarity it seems only a
Couple of weeks since we've ruminated.

Separation
and reunion
vaguely hint
at evolving
personality.

Everyone has issues with family
Or coworkers or friends going on right
Now as somebody's not happy be it
A birthday party that's not wanted or

The disturbance of moving domiciles
Whatever can be wrung through the wringer
Of ceaseless adaptation brutally
And minutely as things are changing for

Better or worse and it's too bad normal
People aren't as sick as alcoholics
Who either disintegrate or practice
Principles to be sober because the

Normally agitated could learn a
Lot from our hilarious bantering.

Every meeting is
a festival of
disruptive
frivolity.

My mom asked about which are the things in
The house that I would like to inherit
And there are many items connected
With memory but I'm at a time when

I'd rather empty my own house of most
Of what I consider as the debris
Of my grown and gone family and I'd
Prefer my living space to embody

A bare simplicity of artful and
Useful implements that are a pleasure
To hold in my hands with the rooms being
An uncluttered arrangement allowing

For the unhindered playing of my mind
Free of the past and untroubled today.

I will take the sturdy
oak rocking chair
that positions
a body
alertly.

My dad used to
sit in the oak chair
rocking watching
football on Sundays.

Everything I do especially the
Composing of pithy poems comes with
A natural human propensity
For measuring and balancing as the

Satisfaction I take in symmetry
Gives me a sense of the mastery of
My surroundings and by assuming the
Task of organizing the lines of words

In ten syllables while also crafting
A flow of rhythm overrunning the
Ends of lines without superfluous words
Brings a feeling of accomplishment as

If I were a finicky mason
Assembling a beautiful wall of stones.

Self-referential
arbitrary choice
emerges into
a regimented
clever expression.

The gesturing of the trees cuts against
The grain of my innate preference for
Measure and symmetry opposing my
Human habits of regularity

With an explosion of angles and crooks
As I gaze at the massive cottonwood
On my corner season after season
And yet the twists and turns of it defy

My comprehension of it as when I
Close my eyes and attempt to capture a
View of it only the vaguest image
Comes to mind as its form surpasses my

Ability to fix and grab ahold
Of — and every single tree is like that.

The trees
grow themselves
wild and
incomprehensible.

The sun is bright this morning after days
Of dominating gray clouds dispensing
Rain and gloom leaving puddles in the low
Areas of my driveway and there are

Hundreds of drops of water hanging from
The crooked branches of my apple tree
With each drop dangling gleaming with sunlight
With the grass glistening reflecting the

Rising sun and though the forecast points to
A continuation of such stormy
And chilly weather for the coming week
Even for a reappearance of snow

Tomorrow buds of leaves are appearing
And the grass is green and growing again.

Clinging gloom on the
undeniable
threshold of spring
moisture brings me
barely suppressed joy.

A sound in the woods is gurgling again
Water is moving over ground again
Collecting itself into creeks and streams
Making its ways along channels down to

The river again clean water coming
From the springs and the saturated earth
Flowing over and around and moving
The smallest of stones about and rounding

The hard edges of the stones persisting
Among the heavy stones and the boulders
Giving the woods a musical patter
Of frolicsome splashing and pouring and

Water has been moving on the earth for
Eons without a lick of memory.

Water doesn't remember
oceans clouds drops
mist fog springs creeks
streams rivers valleys
canyons deltas.

Not every thought I have is worth my time
So many are habitual nonsense
It is an exuberant game to rhyme
Which demands a little reconnaissance
And words resemble a workingman's tools
With usage comes familiarity
It does take practice to master the rules
There is play in verbal dexterity
Mastering facts is the goal of science
And I sprinkle my poems with the truth
Truth and whimsy may make an alliance
Much better than having a wisdom tooth
It is easy to get lost in my head
I'd much rather juggle with words instead.

Every day I am thinking
And my spirits are sinking
But I can waste time
Attempting to rhyme
And I will end up winking.

One is pronounced a hippopotamus
While two are termed as hippopotami
But it's different with rhinoceros
Because we do not say "rhinoceri"
Words are wiggly and they make me weary
There are many ways to spell the vowels
Thankfully we do have dictionaries
Otherwise I would very often scowl
I use the words but didn't invent them
English has become an awful mishmash
What is the logic behind the word "phlegm"?
Thinking too much will summon a whiplash
Who coined the happy word "propitious"?
It is useful for being facetious.

Words are indispensable
They make the world sensible
If I couldn't talk
I would have to squawk
Which isn't delectable.

April in Minnesota is crazy
We just enjoyed days of summery heat
With humidity that made me lazy
Followed by these days of wintery sleet
The buds are growing and the grass is green
I expect that tulips are on the way
The leaves will have an incandescent sheen
But today the sky is a mass of gray
And I am seeing snow on every roof
And my bicycle has gotten a flat
So it's not hard for me to stand aloof
At least we're not swatting at swarming gnats
Temperate weather arrives when it does
April's as crazy as it ever was.

My bicycle tire is fixed
I've ordered new tires
and a bicycle
computer for
mileage and speed.

The news is heavy with tragic events
A police shooting has happened again
Convulsing America with suspense
Because riots are happening again
People are divided by what they see
We are forming into suspicious groups
Our differing narratives don't agree
But who are justified and who are dupes?
Few can counter the tides of history
The Buddha said that the world is burning
Why tragedy comes is a mystery
We are angry and the streets are burning
The best I can do is watch and let go
Society is always full of woe.

I don't know how
liberation comes
but I'm pretty sure
not from anger.

I googled "leafless gutters" because the
Wire mesh isn't keeping the debris
From the trees about my house from clogging
My gutters and I found the website of

A company in Colorado that
Offers leafless gutters and handyman
Services too which I also wanted
Because a bush needs to be removed to

Make way for a downspout that's presently
Blocked leading to water leaking into
My basement so I scheduled a date for
Services and entered my credit card

Information and I was happy that
I had addressed a critical problem.

This morning I am
seized with suspicion
that I used a website
to swindle myself
with naiveté.

I realize the process dispensed with
A meeting with a sales rep who would make
An estimate of the costs and price which
Would be necessary for a proper

Deal and I am seized with revulsion that
I stupidly allowed myself to be
Swindled by a website in cyberspace
Without a telephone number so I

Call my credit card company and learn
That the charge hasn't yet happened and with
Relief I cancel the card to stop the
Payment redeeming my ineptitude —

I only wasted time in frustration
In which I could have written poetry.

I could have
written wonderful
poetry if I hadn't
been distracted.

By myself on the way to Amsterdam
I remember the White Cliffs of Dover
Taking the ferry and the trains and trams
I found a love I've not gotten over
Inside of a book of Shakespeare's sonnets
I was a lonely student at Oxford
Seeking love in solitary moments
Feeling emotions that didn't accord
I was piqued by his pitiful laments
By his lusty and cloying strategy
And by his utterly sincere pretense
With metaphorical rascality
But most of all I loved his playful words
And everything else was kind of absurd.

I admired the hearty
way Shakespeare had
of making words flow
and resonate.

Shakespeare was a superior playwright
But in sonnets he became an actor
Assuming the role of a lover's plight
Striking poses of impassioned fracture
He was in love with someone much younger
And much lamented his impending death
Implying unappeasable hunger
Dreading the expiration of his breath
He contrived to make his lover guilty
By pretending to let his lover go
Slighting himself — soliciting pity
And then he turned to braggadocio
Deploying all the tricks that words can do
Plotting to finagle a rendezvous.

While I waited for a train
in Amsterdam Shakespeare
cast a spell on me.

I could let my mind drift away with clouds
They are wispy and moving south today
They often cover the sky like a shroud
But I could let the clouds take me away
The trees are an enticing counterpoint
Without a wind they stand so peacefully
They're an infinity of crooks and joints
They are expressing themselves quietly
I love to watch the procession of light
Seeing contrails of a jetliner drift
It's easy to discount the joys of sight
And to forget that my eyes are a gift
But so much thinking goes on in my head
I get stuck in controversy instead.

I am not free of
the compulsion
to organize myself
and make decisions.

I'd rather not be guarded with my words
Because I love easy conversation
But it's true I am a bit of a nerd
And can't meet everyone's expectations
With certain people I discuss the news
But with some those topics are out of bounds
Because we have to share similar views
Otherwise there's too much trouble around
If you ask me I'll tell you what I think
And I'm sure it would be enjoyable
It is joyous to find ourselves in sync
But first I'd like you to be flexible
I don't insist that we need to agree
But I desire the grace to be carefree.

With some people
I can sense a brick wall
existing behind
their eyes.

Saturday is an oasis for me
When I sit at my desk writing poems
Being as nonsensical as I please
Typing my lines of rambunctious hokum
I had a girlfriend much smarter than me
I would visit her about once a week
But we couldn't agree ultimately
So now we're separate and we don't speak
I don't really know what happened that day
Suddenly she was unhappy with me
I expect I'll find another someday
One who's much less complicated maybe
Saturday is free — I do what I want
It's easy for me to be nonchalant.

Shakespeare made
such a big deal out of love
but I am suspicious —
was it all an act?

So much of life is indescribable
There is only so much that words can do
The forms of the trees are ineffable
Can't always explain what I think is true
The sun and the clouds are quite beautiful
But can't exactly articulate why
Consciousness is incomprehensible
I try to think but my thoughts go awry
Will I go to sleep and never wake up?
Did I come to the earth from somewhere else?
I am confused — will I ever grow up?
Is this all that there is — with nothing else?
How much am I free to think what I want?
I can relax with a buttered croissant.

A single cloud is
transforming in
the sky at a
gentle pace.

Let these pages enfold my memory
I don't want to feel the weight anymore
I don't remember very cleverly
What I recall I would rather ignore
What stands out is painful experience
All the things that I would like to forget
All the disappointed reminiscence
Let me skillfully use the alphabet
I will give my essence to these pages
Let my memory be within this book
And let the book be the one that ages
I can fashion out a witty scrapbook
I want to be smartly spontaneous
Like the sky itself — momentaneous.

The sky doesn't remember
yesterday as it's awake and
liberated.

Actors know the power of their faces
They reflect the subtlest emotions
Sincerity and empathy graces
Expressing that which remains unspoken
They say so much with a cast of their eyes
Summoning pity with tremulous lips
Utterly convincing when telling lies
It's hard to believe they're following scripts
They must embody emotions themselves
Feeling the sadness and disappointment
Adopting the aggressions that compel
With authenticity being poignant
I have to wonder who they really are
Doing what's needed to become a star.

The best actors
don't overplay
but genuinely
express what's
put on.

Do I really desire to fall in love?
Or is it best to encourage friendship?
Do I want a lover's passion? Sort of
Perhaps it's best to have companionship
But do I want the grip of obsession?
I know what it's like to become consumed
Nagging jealousy comes with possession
A desperate attachment is perfumed
Observe what love did to William Shakespeare
Love made him gesticulate like a fool
Emotions are hard — especially fear
And rejection can seem utterly cruel
So I don't know what will happen to me
And all I can do is to wait and see.

Romantic love
isn't gentle — it's
like being run over
by a Mack truck.

Kitcat is expert at rascality
But I can't say that he's a deep thinker
He likes to show off his dexterity
When evading my grasp he's a slinker
He's crafty at grabbing my attention
He'll knock containers off the kitchen counter
Then he'll look at me with expectation
Wanting to spark a nutty encounter
But I don't chase I just expostulate
I stay on the couch while waving my arms
I'm often pretending to be irate
But I'm sure that he knows I mean no harm
He's not very brainy but is a clown
Making me grateful that he is around.

While he lays on his back
we slap and swat
hands and paws
and he tries to bite
while I sing nonsense.

They often come about the size of peas
But once in a while they're elephantine
Then I am surprised and certainly pleased
So weighty with juice and tasting so fine
They're shipped to America from Chile
Which really is a modern miracle
They're not necessary — but are frilly
And they do make my breakfast magical
I combine their flavor with banana
I do love my exotic morning fruit
I sprinkle both upon my granola
They give my appetite a mighty toot
They come here — even in February
What would I do without my blueberries?

The skim milk
that completes
the ensemble is
pleasingly
bland.

Early in the morning while passing an
Ash tree I notice about a dozen
Turkey vultures at the top of a tree
With several of them spreading out their wings

And I observe that that particular
Tree that I pass every day has about
It a disheveled appearance because
Its branches and twigs are extending in

A weirdly chaotic fashion — so here
Are these strange birds with a six-foot wingspan
Gathered together quietly perching
In an odd-looking tree and I don't know

What the birds are thinking but I'm amazed
To see such an assemblage of beings.

When I keep my eyes open
and my mind quiet
even in my own
neighborhood the
world surprises me.

Imagine being a photon of light
Zipping away from a supernova
Exhalation of energy at the
Speed of light — I wonder whether as a

Particular particle I would have
A sensation of motion noticing
Galaxies zooming by for billions of
Years with neither acceleration nor

Diminution of impetus or would
There be an absence of a sense of time
As my arriving and departing are
Simultaneous instantaneous

As there would no longer be time or space
For a ham sandwich and a tomato.

In
reality
my
neighborhood
is
odd.

Might I politely have your attention
And persuade you to come together with
Me skipping along over syllables
Lazily and lackadaisically

As I hint at a truth advantageous
And propitious for you to absorb
Not that I'm the only person privy
To the inside scoop as it's a fact as

Common as a heartbeat as it's a trick
Of directing oneself away from the
Habituated run of the mind so
Often chewing over useless thinking

Serving only for agitation — you
Should be wary of knowing the news.

The news isn't
only informing
but also skewing
opinions and
emotions.

I'm not an advocate of ignorance
As the human mind is incapable
Of avoiding the cultivation of
Opinions which quite naturally are

Prickly and neither am I bestowing
Wishy-washy attitudes upon you
As we can't help digging into things as
Determinedly as a wiener dog but

I am reminding myself and also
Suggesting to you it's good at times to
Lovingly propagate the emptiness
Of the sky allowing the thunderclouds

And lightning due exercise while also
Remaining open and spontaneous.

The open sky
receives the weather
of the world but
holds on to
nothing.

In the grip of daily habit I drive
About Stillwater letting the chatter
Of the radio provide me with the
Political opinion that I like

Aware of the toxicity coming
With my opinions of issues over
Which I have no measure of influence
And I often become weary as the

Controversy never ceases and for
An escape I've taken to observing
The various posturing of the trees
As a tonic and an antidote as

They are visions of spontaneity
Separate from human contrivances.

Trees do have
patterns of specie
but they are
infinitely
various.

When my energy wanes and peters out
My attitude is unreliable
I discover myself consumed with doubt
My ambitions are unbelievable
Then I compare my progress with others
Seeing I lack the friends that many have
That I haven't had my share of lovers
And then my battered ego needs a salve
But this has happened many times before
I know such thoughts are unreliable
So I don't debate myself anymore
And harmony is unsustainable
Energy naturally ebbs and flows
I don't punish myself when I am low.

Surfing
melancholy
is easier.

I am out of step with fashion today
Poets now are revolutionary
I don't want the outrage that they convey
Prefer to avoid verbal savagery
I do not believe in collective guilt
Quite distrust their poisonous narratives
I'd rather compose a different script
Can't be so resolutely negative
But poets are out of fashion also
No one reads poetry much anymore
Can poets make money? I don't think so
We aren't celebrated in the bookstores
Don't really care that I'm out of fashion
I write poetry for satisfaction.

I
love
to
make
the
words
dance.

Does Shakespeare comport with Japanese Zen?
Elizabethan poems are wordy
The bard wrote with honeyed metaphors then
English poetry is much more heady
The Japanese are sparing with their words
They don't invest so much in verbiage
And yet they are effective with their verbs
They slice delusion with a razor's edge
Zen is a practice based on clarity
And Japanese poetry is concise
I admire Shakespeare's dexterity
And in his wordiness he is precise
Emulating both may just be crazy
Whatever I do can't be lazy.

I adore
Matsuo
Basho's
frog jumping
into a temple
pond.

I do my best to be open to life
To forget the burdens of yesterday
To forge of myself a very keen knife
And slice through the troubles along my way
But I know I can't function on my own
That life is better when someone loves me
That people don't prosper living alone
That it is healthy for us to agree
I want to grasp hold of true perceptions
And to minimize my own disturbance
To take ownership of my selections
To be balanced in every occurrence
We are thrust on the point of becoming
And something propitious is coming.

I can't see
around corners
and can only
clarify me.

I am grateful to see hypocrisy
As it shows me clearly what not to do
Some are brazen in their mendacity
But it's sometimes hard to see as I do
Opinions vary and we don't agree
We come at things from various angles
That it's hard to know the truth — I concede
Omniscience is given to angels
There is a tinge to denunciations
A tactile hint of falsification
Making me question their accusations
They are broadcasting a mad delusion
And the hypocrites are always angry
Which sooner or later summons gangrene.

A person has to watch
for contradictory
behavior over time
to spot hypocrisy.

The sky has the virtue of emptiness
Its true quality is invisible
Its conversion is instantaneous
Always spontaneously flexible
A cloudless sky isn't really empty
The life of the sunlight is pouring down
Soliciting oxygen from the trees
The stars are visible after sundown
And winter is often shrouded with clouds
Then the earth is saturated with rain
And in summer the thunderheads resound
In every season sunlight comes again
But the sky itself is not the weather
It's the emptiness holding the weather.

The cosmos is not
galaxies and time
it is emptiness holding
galaxies and time.

In the winter I wrote about tulips
Because it's good to be optimistic
So I imagined the blooming tulips
Lifting my mood by being artistic
It's been a chilly and a dreary spring
Had I known I'd have been disappointed
I can't predict what the future will bring
It's very easy to be downhearted
But it's rainy today and I don't care
I am even quite enthusiastic
What comes today I can easily bear
I am doing spiritual gymnastics
Cavorting with words will lighten my mood
Without playing tricks my life would be skewed.

By the garage
today I see
red and yellow tulips
come up simultaneously
with daffodils.

In Washington D.C. cherry trees bloom
During the warm early days of April
But how can anyone escape the gloom
At the site of national betrayal?
In Japan they celebrate plum blossoms
That appear in February and March
They are such sweet and delicate blossoms
When beauty and the end of winter merge
And in Japan they enjoy Golden Week
Which happens within the first week of May
Everyone celebrates which is unique
As the cherry blossoms brighten their days
And also in May wisteria comes
When purple flowers exquisitely bloom.

The Japanese bestowed
the gift of cherry trees
on Washington D.C. —
the city of our
political disease.

Most of April has been damp and soggy
Puddles are collecting on my driveway
My apple trees are barren and gnarly
They don't blossom until the end of May
Giving me something to look forward to
I've mowed the lawn but it's growing slowly
And outside now I don't have much to do
At least it's unlikely to be snowy
I love my lilac bush and apple trees
When they bloom I quietly celebrate
And I welcome seeing the bumblebees
Spring comes in Minnesota — it's not late
My wiry lilac bush and apple trees
Determinedly persist through the deep freeze.

In late May the scent
of lilac and apple
blossoms mingle
over my yard
for about a week.

A downpour spattering on the concrete
Along with bamboo knocking together
Such a welcome release from sticky heat
That all these years later I remember
We were lying near the open window
Wrapped in warm blankets upon our futons
A married couple living in Kyoto
With so much youthful drama going on
It's a memory of a vanished time
Of the sensations that return to me
Of my own emotional pantomime
Remembering is important to me
There was so much life ahead of us then
I'd love to have the time over again.

Some
memories
abide
and I
don't know
why.

The alphabet is sophisticated
It gives the language organization
Sounds and meanings can be regulated
With dictionaries for definitions
Takes so much time to get educated
I've learned the grammatical conventions
A thrust of culture is indicated
A system aiding my comprehension
Eventually I've graduated
Discover myself in competition
Our society is complicated
Producing a little hypertension
I admit to my share of pretension
And I may even foster dissension.

Gazing at the
wild gesticulation
of the trees is an
antidote to
human thought.

How do you measure your velocity?
Do you enjoy an appetite for speed?
Do you have time for curiosity?
Is finishing early a worthy need?
Who could resist youthful precocity?
Is desire unambiguously greed?
What is the source of generosity?
Do you embody unknowable seeds?
Is there advantage in ferocity?
What does an obsessive ambition feed?
What is the goal of reciprocity?
Does genuine unselfish love succeed?
Is there any use in loquacity?
Or is it only harmless verbosity?

You may think you are
stationary but really
you are moving at
one thousand miles an hour
rotating upon the earth.

I admire a writer who scolded me
He was a professor but gave it up
He's intelligent and can be cranky
He loves literature with no letup
With his family he moved to Vermont
Choosing to live a simple farming life
A genuinely naïve dilettante
They struggled to survive — he and his wife
They started out as hippie homesteaders
Indulging whimsy — not experience
Now they are clever and weathered farmers
Overcoming hardships with resilience
All his life he's been writing and reading
And I find his opinions compelling.

I disparaged rhyming
and he chided me
remarking rhyming makes
remembering poetry
easier.

I dislike the revolutionaries
Because of their conceit that they know best
Believing as they do that every age
That existed before their enlightened

Presence is unworthy of memory
While I rejoice in watching the classic
"Casablanca" starring Humphrey Bogart
And Ingrid Bergman depicting a love

Frustrated and foregone amid the turns
Of a world war when America and
The Allies were confronting the Nazi
Menace that was a genuine threat to

Civilization during the days when
We could be proud to be American.

Listening to
Roger Ebert's expert
commentary brought
the artistry and times
to life.

On a solitary Sunday I was happy
To watch a documentary on a
Spicy slice of Americana that
Some today would label the "toxic

Masculinity" of professional
Wrestling in which the enormously
Musclebound wresters bellow and toss
Each other about which isn't my cup

Of tea but my learning of the life
Of the seven-foot-four — five-hundred pound —
World-famous but mostly misunderstood
Andre the Giant was poignant as he

Was always traveling and forgoing a
Family life and was in constant pain.

He died at forty-six
and celebrity came
with a price but he
did what he thought
God intended.

In imitation of the guardians
At the gates before Buddhist temples in
Japan my half-Japanese daughter sewed
Together with herringbone fabric two

Foxes posed in suitably contrasting
Sitting postures with demonic red eyes
Which my ex-wife and I — my daughter and
Her husband — and their Chinese friend — had the

Happy occasion to view inside of
The entrance to the museum of the
Minneapolis Academy of
Art and Design where my daughter's foxes

Are being honored for their quality —
And I am the proudest guy in the town.

Jocelyn connects
so much of what
I love from the past
going forward.

Yao — my Daughter's friend and fellow artist
From China — is calmly observant as
We are having Japanese cuisine in
A restaurant in Minneapolis

When I learn that she animated a
Colorful and exquisitely drawn book
Featuring my son-in-law Eric who
Is eating with us depicting Eric

As a lovably round cartoon figure
Who has a job answering phone calls from
Distressed people with Eric consoling
Them and as he does over the pages

A blue liquid composing the tears of
Sorrow transfer from callers to Eric.

Eric ends up sloshing
inside with tears of
sorrow — artists are
observant.

The distance in the night is palpable
When a train's horn intones its mournful sound
Over the fields and grasses and the woods
Outside of the city alerting me

To the heavy vibration of a line
Of cars throbbing and throbbing in the dark
And it's difficult to determine the
Direction and the distance of the train —

I only know that someone is driving
Somewhere as I listen for the rumble
Of an engine that's hard to distinguish
In the happenstance moment that I step

Outside of my house on a night when I
Woke and had trouble getting back to sleep.

Perhaps only deer
crows foxes and
coyotes are
listening.

There is a reliable moment in
The morning when my noggin dispenses
With lingering drowsiness and becomes
Alert when I'm finished with my chores and

Enter into the sanctuary of
My little bathroom to shave and shower
And beyond the ritual of using
The razor I don't attend much to my

Image because I've seen it all before
But the moment pops with inspiration
As I get glimpses of insight outside
Of the narrow confines of habits and

I grasp spontaneously light-hearted
Ways of articulating new meaning.

With the softness
of the towel that I wrap
around myself
I dry the water drops
dappling my back.

My lilac bush
and apple trees
are leafing out
gradually amid
rainy days.

—*Tekkan*

www.ingramcontent.com/pod-product-compliance
Lightning Source LLC
Chambersburg PA
CBHW040419100526
44589CB00021B/2754